The Emotionally Unavailable Man

A Blueprint for Healing

—A Book for Men—

Patti Henry, M.Ed., L.P.C.

Rainbow Books, Inc. ❖ Florida

Library of Congress Cataloging-In-Publication Data

Henry, Patti, 1956-
    The emotionally unavailable man : a blueprint for healing / Patti Henry.
        p. cm.
    Includes index.
    ISBN 1-56825-096-7 (trade softcover : alk. paper)
1. Men—Psychology. I. Title.
    HQ1090.H46 2004
    158.2—dc22

                                              2004008252

The Emotionally Unavailable Man: A Blueprint for Healing
© 2004 by Patti Henry, M.Ed., L.P.C. (www.patti-henry.com)
ISBN 1-56825-096-7

Published by
    Rainbow Books, Inc., P. O. Box 430, Highland City, FL 33846-0430
Editorial Offices and Wholesale/Distributor Orders
    Telephone: (863) 648-4420
    Email: RBIbooks@aol.com
Individuals' Orders
    Toll-free Telephone (800) 431-1579
    http://www.AllBookStores.com

∞The paper used in this publication meets the minimum requirements of the American National Standard for Information Sciences—Permanence of Paper for Printed Library Materials, ANSI Z39.48–1984.

First edition 2004
10 09 08 07 06 05 04 5 4 3 2 1
Printed in the United States of America

For Jeff

Permissions

Man's Search for Meaning by Viktor Frankl, is published by Beacon Press.

The Onion Field by Joseph Wambaugh, is published by Dell Publishing, a division of Random House, Inc.

The Prophet by Kahlil Gibran, is published by Alfred A. Knopf, a division of Random House, Inc.

"TIME Person of the Year," *TIME* © 2001 TIME, Inc., reprinted by permission.

Men's Book Contents

Acknowledgments

Every book has its story. This one goes like this:

I was writing a book when suddenly it occurred to me that I was writing the wrong book. So, I set that manuscript aside, and this one walked in fully intact. Within 15 minutes the complete outline, chapter by chapter, was down on paper. So, first I thank God.

I began writing. With a busy practice, it was hard for me to find the hours I needed to concentrate. So, I set aside 15 hours a week just for this book. I thank my sister and my brother-in-law, Valerie and Kit Carson Smith, who sent me checks for the next six months to pay for those writing hours, so I didn't have to worry about money. Without their financial and emotional backing, this book would not have been possible.

I wrote for four months. My father died. I couldn't concentrate for about six weeks, but when I came back to the manuscript, a new freedom came with me. Somehow I felt my dad's encouragement to write. So, I thank my dad, in a way, for dying. Because in death I believe he received enlightenment and, somehow, that helped me. It reinforced to me how important it was to write this book.

I wrote for two more months. I didn't talk about it much to anyone, but my family quietly supported me: eating lots of takeout, helping with the chores, and not asking how it was going. So, I thank my two boys, Scott and Eric, plus my husband, Jeff, who is my rock, for all their quiet, thorough love, support, and understanding.

Then one day I wrote the last sentence and the last period. I cried.

It was like birthing a baby. I gave my manuscript to my husband with the instructions, "Don't tell me anything negative. Only positives. I can't handle anything negative yet." He honored that. And then we went through it again — and again — and again, each time delving a bit more into honest criticism. He has been my very gentle editor throughout the whole rewriting process. I cannot say thank you enough to him or to God for him.

Next I asked trusted friends, family, and colleagues to read the manuscript and give me feedback, all of which was invaluable. I thank and respectfully acknowledge each of them: my mom and stepfather, Donna and Ernie Holmes; my friends and colleagues: Ruth Arnold, Mona Chamberlain, Woody Forrieter, Karl Weston, Audrey Anastasia, Bill Taube, Susan Herbold, Sylvia Westlake, Bill Clendenen, Joanna Crawford, Wendy Schumer, Heloise Lynn, Fred Crawford, Liz Steele, Amy Gurghigian, Bitsy Cleveland, Kay Schlembach, Michael Marcoux, Ken Bielicki, and Jim Dickinson. Thank you.

Next came the time for the final rewrite and research. For this I received unbelievable amounts of support and encouragement every step along the way. I wish to thank Otto Fad, animal trainer at Sea World in Florida; Bonnie and Troy, assistants at the Houston Civil Court House; Newton Hightower, author of *Anger Busting 101*; and Dr. Reverend Johnny Ray Youngblood, an incredible human being whose energy and belief in me has been life-giving.

Then last, but not least, was my search for a publisher. I must confess, I sent my manuscript to only one: Rainbow Books, Inc. They sent me an offer. We negotiated a bit, wrestled a bit, laughed a bit, and then came to terms. I thank Betty Wright, senior publisher at Rainbow, for being so easy to work with, so full of wisdom, and such a delight.

My acknowledgments would not be complete, however, without mentioning all the clients I have had the honor and privilege to work with over the years. I salute you. I salute your courage. Daily you inspire me and I thank you.

Introduction

Emotional work is like running a marathon. No one can do it for you. You can have a coach, you can have a running partner, you can have friends cheering you on, you can even drink water at every water station, but *you* have to do the running. You have to make the commitment. You have to put one foot in front of the other if you want to finish the race.

May the words in this book give you the encouragement you need to go the distance.

Chapter 1

A Disadvantage

Ever feel like a little boy in a grown up body? As a psychotherapist in private practice, I hear this complaint often. I am writing this book because of it. Men keep coming to my office, one after another, hurting, wounded, defended, but mostly, unhappy. Doctors, lawyers, engineers, bus drivers, salesmen, postmen, business owners, multi-millionaires and men that are broke. It doesn't matter. They all have the same story. Though the words and the details vary greatly, the bottom line is always the same: they have very little sense of self and very little sense of personal power. They feel like they are trapped, dying somehow. They feel like little boys in grown up bodies.

The good news is men are *coming* to my office. Ten years ago, 5-10 percent of my clients were men. Now, I'm seeing 50-60 percent men. Men searching. Men wanting answers. Men wanting to be happy. I assume you must be searching, too, or you wouldn't be reading this book. Or at least your wife or girlfriend feels you need to be searching, so you are reading this book. Either way, you're reading this book, which is great. I hope you find some answers here.

My theory — and it is just a theory based on working with hundreds of clients over the years — is that the problem for men begins with how they were treated as boys. Our culture has a long-standing tradition of teaching our little boys to cut off from their feelings. I think this is damaging to them. This makes them emotionally unavailable to themselves as well as others. It shuts down a huge part of their psyches and *stunts their emotional development*. They, therefore, get stuck at a young age of emotional development. No wonder men so often express this concern of still feeling like a little boy. Think about it. What were you taught to do with your emotions? Especially painful ones. Men tell me that they were taught:

- Big boys don't cry.
- Don't be a sissy.
- Emotions mean you're weak.
- Stop crying or I'll give you something to cry about.
- Be a man.
- You're a baby (a crybaby, a wimp, a girl, an embarrassment to the family, not my son, etc.).

Any of these messages sound familiar to you? Let me give you an example. When my oldest son was 10, he played in a basketball league with 9 and 10 year olds. There was one 9 year old on his team who was very tiny. There was one 10 year old on the other team who was the opposite of tiny. In fact I'd never seen a 10 year old this big before. At one point little Tiny was "guarding" Mr. Big. Well, Mr. Big decided to go in for a basket and literally ran over little Tiny. Plowed him to the ground and ran him over. The little boy's head cracked against the gym floor and he lay in the fetal position, clutching his side, crying, writhing in pain. The gym fell completely silent — except for the little boy's mother who was screaming from the bleachers, "Suck it up, son! Suck it up!"

Maybe *your* mom gave *you* that message. Suck it up. Maybe your dad. Maybe both. I don't know. All I know is: that little boy curled up in a ball on the basketball floor was hurting. Physically. Emotionally. At some level he must have been struggling between trying to please his mother and not embarrass her, and being true to his experience of pain. I'll bet, eventually, his mother wins out and our world will have one more little boy who has learned not to feel. How about you? What happened to you?

What, too, has happened to our country? Haven't we been teaching this to our little boys for hundreds of years? It worked before for men — so why isn't it working now?

Because times have changed. When? I would say during World War II. Why? Because that is when women joined the work force en masse. Before that, men and women both had their own sort of advantages. Women had their emotional selves which men knew little or nothing about, and men had their work world, which women knew little or nothing about. Furthermore, men's work world did not challenge them emotionally because it was filled with MEN. However, when women joined the work force all of that began to slowly but surely change. Suddenly, women were ever so slightly privy to the man's secret world, and they came equipped with emotions, too.

Now, fast forward until today, the 21st century. According to the Center for Women's Business Research, as of 2002, there were an estimated 6.2 *million* women-owned firms in the United States, employing 9.2 million people and generating $1.15 trillion in sales. Furthermore, 63 million women were employed outside of the home, while 81 percent of all single parent families were headed by them.

The point is, women seem to have gained some advantage over the last 60 years. They have their emotions — little girls are not taught to cut off from that part of themselves — and they have the business world, too. Men, however, have arrived somewhat at a disadvantage. They have the business world. Period. Having been taught to cut off from their emotional selves as little boys, they often blunder in the emotional arena. They are afraid/confused/repulsed/threatened when women *feel*. To this women have not responded kindly. They are angry, frustrated, feel cheated, and so often openly express their disdain and disrespect of men (I mean, there are *greeting cards* one after another that tout the "men are jerks" theme!). With this men seem to have developed a deep, often unconscious, sense of insecurity.

Now, please note, I am talking in very generalized terms. This isn't true of ALL men, and of course, there are certainly many exceptions to every rule. But it does seem to me that, in general, men are coming to my office broken, wounded, scared, and quite frankly, beaten up, because women have the power in their lives. Men do not seem to have the tools to deal with emotional, feeling women, and yet women do have the tools to deal with men both emotionally and in the business world.

In summary, my theory is that men are at a disadvantage. My belief is that men need healing. My belief is that men need help getting reconnected to their emotional selves so that they can take their *whole* selves with them into a marriage or into the work place or wherever. Just like women get to do.

Chapter 2

The Hurricane

I also believe women have a big part in men's emotional unavailability. That's why there are two sides to this book. Women, unwittingly I think, tend to perpetuate men's little boy "stuck." Consider this quote from one of my clients:

"My wife says I don't talk. I don't communicate. But when I try to talk to her, it's as if I hold up my tea cup for a cup of water and she hits me with a tidal wave. So I just shut up. And then she beats me up some more — for not talking!"

I call this the hurricane. It is a term coined in Mira Kirshenbaum's book, *Too Good to Leave, Too Bad to Stay*. In her book, the author paints this great image of a person outside in a hurricane trying to walk *against* the direction the wind is blowing. Having lived in Houston through a category three hurricane, I can personally attest to what Ms. Kirshenbaum describes: to succeed at getting from point A to point B facing 125 m.p.h. gusts is almost impossible. My experience was, at 105 pounds, it *was* impossible. It took every ounce of energy I had to go a few steps into the wind only to be pushed back suddenly by a forceful gust. It didn't take long for me to decide my idea of going from point A to point B against this ferocious wind was crazy. It was just too hard. I didn't have enough power to conquer that wind! I gave up. I decided point A would have to do because it was as far as I could go.

Now translate that into emotional terms. If a man who has been taught to cut off from his emotions as so many, many men have been taught, encounters a wife or a girlfriend or a parent or a boss who starts cranking up the emotional hurricane, that same powerless feeling occurs. It's overwhelming. It's defeating. It's crazy to go against that kind of force. He doesn't have the tools he would need to deal with all that emotion. He doesn't have his emotional self available to compete successfully in an emotional environment. He gives up. Retreats. Or in some cases, runs for his life.

Let me give you an example. Years ago when I was working in a very small town in Germany, a friend came to visit. She didn't speak German at all but was eager to explore the town nonetheless. She set off early in the morning while I went to work. At some point she decided to call her husband in America to chat with him of her adventures. She went to the post office to make a public call which was great thinking. However, the German phone system, unbeknownst to my friend, was different than the American phone system. In America, you dialed the number you were calling and then punched in your credit card number to put it on your credit card. In Germany, you had to contact an operator to put it on your card or else pay the post office in cash. My friend, being an American, did it the American way. Her husband's number first, credit card number second. As soon as her husband's number was entered, however, the call connected and did not even register the credit card number that was being punched in. So there lie the problem. My friend felt confident she had put the call on her credit card. The post office manager, however, felt equally confident that she owed him 104 Deutsche marks for the call (about $54). He stopped her as she was leaving the building. She was, like many men in emotional situations, ill-equipped. She did not have the tools needed to adequately communicate her point. She kept saying credit card and the manager kept saying money. She took the credit card out to show him and he pointed to the traveler's checks in her wallet. At that point he took her firmly by the arm, walked her out the door, down the street, and into the bank. There he urged her to give a traveler's check to the banker. Emotionally exhausted and feeling humiliated, she relented. The banker gave her $46 in marks and the postal manager his rightfully deserved $54 worth. By the time she made it back across town where I was, she was furious. She felt that she had been ripped off royally, of course.

She had experienced that sense of powerlessness. She did not have the verbal tools she needed to get the manager to understand. She felt at his mercy. This, too, is the plight of many men when they find themselves in an emotional arena with few, if any, tools at hand. They either grab an ineffective tool or stand there silent, powerless, defeated — both of which, unfortunately, just fuel the hurricane.

So what does a hurricane look like? The hurricane can be tears. Sobs, excruciating hurt. The hurricane can be rage. Screaming, throwing, name calling, verbal abuse. The hurricane can be a mixture of several intense emotions. Hurt, anger, fear, disappointment, frustration. The hurricane can be incessant talking, nagging, ranting and raving. It can be the cold shoulder, silence, stomping around slamming the cabinet doors. The point is, the hurricane takes many forms, but the bottom line is this: it is powerful and it is relentless.

I've had men tell me:

- I feel emasculated by it.
- I feel terrified like my life is at risk.
- I feel battered and then ashamed.
- I feel totally without any power. There is nothing I can do to shut it off.
- I feel enraged by it. Sometimes I even hit her to shut her up.
- I feel so frustrated by it. It's like I'm invisible and she can't see me.
- It is completely overwhelming. I just shut down.

I do a lot of marriage counseling. What amazes me is that within five minutes of the first session I can tell who has the power in the relationship. Nine times out of ten, it's the woman. This is my test. I ask one question making it clear that I need an answer from each of them. My question is: "What is your marriage like for you?" And then I say, "It doesn't matter who answers first." At this point, the husband and wife look at each other and the wife so often says, "You go first." And he does! No discussion, no questions asked. That's a little red flag I take note of.

There are, of course, some variations to this theme of a direct order from the wife. Sometimes it's accompanied by a put-down. That's a *big* red flag I take note of. "You go first. *This* ought to be interesting." I've even had wives say to me, "I'll go first. He doesn't talk." Then they take off into a long monologue of how inadequate their partner is and how unfulfilling the marriage is for them. Then I know where we stand. The wife has the power. The husband is scrambling. He's been beaten up emotionally and is probably responding like a little boy in this marriage.

Which never works. It just brings on the hurricane.

When the wife continues to be in charge of the session and go on and on and on, my next question is directed at the husband. "Did you have a parent that raged or was extremely powerful in one way or another?" He looks at me astounded and says incredulously, "Yes, I did. How did you know that?" I have to chuckle because I am not a fortune teller. The reality is: it's predictable. The husband is used to this pattern. He has seen it before. I know, too, that he learned somewhere along the way to keep his mouth shut, to cut off from expressing any feelings, and that emotions aren't safe. What happened to you?

Power Parents

Were you raised by a power person? Power people are people who have an enormous amount of power — a disproportionate amount of power — in the family system. They are the hurricanes. The family system often, but not always, revolves around them. There are, of course, many faces to this. I will give you some examples that I have heard in my sessions, but know that this list is not at all complete. You will need to consider your own parents and try to honestly assess if one or both of them was a power person. Some people know right away:

- Definitely my mom was a power person. She was a control FREAK.
- My father. He was an alcoholic and he was a mean alcoholic.
- My mom. She owned her own company and *nobody* messed with her.
- My mom. She called all the shots. My dad was just quiet and took it.
- My dad was a rager. We were all scared of him.
- My dad. If you didn't do what he wanted, how he wanted, he just cut you off. Ignored you. That was the worst.

Other Stories:

- I could never really get my dad's approval. No matter what I did, it wasn't good enough. He'd find some way to make you feel like an A should have been an A+ or an A+ should have been an A++. He always kept raising the bar, and I could never reach it.
- I never thought of my mother as a power person because she was sick my whole life. Everything revolved around whether or not Mom was feeling good enough to do something if we did it or not. And we just knew to be quiet and good. She had enough to deal with.
- My father was a sociopath. And a millionaire. It was as if I didn't count unless he could show me off like a trophy. He didn't care about me — he cared about how I made him look.
- My father's love was definitely conditional. If you acted a certain way and did the right thing — which was whatever it was *he* wanted — then you were the greatest. Otherwise, he raged.

- My mother had an explosive anger. You never knew what would set her off.

- We had to always clean up the house before my father got home from work because as soon as he got home he did an "inspection." Believe you me, you didn't want to fail the inspection.

- When something broke in our house — even by accident — my mother would get scared and make us kids promise not to tell our dad. Sometimes we'd even make up a story together to tell him so he wouldn't get mad at her.

- My mother was so weird. It was embarrassing. I could never bring any of my friends home. You never knew what she'd do next.

- My parents were real religious. You didn't sass, drink, smoke, cuss, or even *say* the word sex. If you did my dad would give you a whooping you'd never forget. The irony is, I found out my dad used to go to prostitutes all the time.

- My mother ruled our house with guilt. She guilted you about everything.

- My dad used to tell us, don't upset your mother. Just go to your room when she gets like that. Basically he was telling us don't have a voice. Swallow it.

- My father was a doctor. He was the first in our family and my mother adored him. I always felt so selfish when I wanted him to spend time with me. My mother told me that he had patients who were dying and that *they* needed him.

- My dad never said anything. He ignored us even when we talked to him. He was a nonentity. My mother ran the house.

The list goes on and on and on. The point is, a little boy raised with a power parent feels small and powerless. He is often afraid of the parent or tries desperately to please him or her. The power parent seems larger than life. There is no use trying to negotiate because the power parent always wins.

A large part of the damage that happens to a little boy in this system is that he gets used to it. He gets used to keeping his mouth shut, not rocking the boat, and staying out of the hurricane's way. He learns that this is the way life IS. This child often goes emotionally underground early on: just to survive. He lives a very active internal life but learns to keep his mouth shut. He learns to respond the way he needs to respond to stay safe. He learns to suck it up.

And I say thank goodness for that. Kids really are victims in a hurricane/power person system and really have very little, if any, power to change things. They have to cope any way they can. What happens, though, to this little boy when he grows up?

Chapter 3

Avoiding the Hurricane

First of all, as this little boy grows up he learns that he has two main options to survive: fight or flight. Either to fight like hell against the hurricane (the best defense is a good offense) or to avoid it (go underground). He learns how to *react* to the system. He does not learn how to have authentic power in the system. He does not learn how to change the system. He doesn't even learn that the system is changeable.

So, as you begin this chapter, I want to start with saying, if you were that little boy, give yourself some grace as you continue reading. You learned what you learned, and you didn't learn what you weren't taught. Chances are you don't speak Chinese either. Why? Because no one taught you Chinese. Similarly, no one taught you how to have authentic power around the hurricane, and no one taught you how to change the system. Okay, so you didn't get those tools. So what? Be gentle with yourself. You didn't get Chinese either. It's not your fault. You weren't taught them because your parents probably didn't have them to give. That's what this book is about. Keep reading. My hope for you is that you will get the tools you need here.

Again, be gentle with yourself. Give yourself grace. I say give yourself grace because when you start to look at what you do to cope with the hurricane it can be kind of an embarrassing realization. It's somewhat humiliating to take a good honest look at the behaviors you learned as a little boy that you are still employing as an adult man. At least with my clients I go gently with them through this step. Let's face it, it's humbling to realize you are using a five year old's coping mechanisms at 30, 40, 50 years old.

So go gently, and let's look at these coping mechanisms as they translate into adult behaviors. Remember, there are two basic mechanisms: flight (avoidance) or fight. Avoid the hurricane because hurricanes are scary and you can't have fear because then you are a sissy. Or, fight like hell against the hurricane to prove to yourself and others that you don't have fear and therefore are not a sissy. Unfortunately, both of these "choices," are really just reactions and carry no authentic power.

Let's look closer at the avoidance coping mechanism. Keep in mind that there are LOTS of ways to avoid the hurricane, and I will not touch on them all here. These are simply some of the more prevalent avoidance techniques.

Flight

Any "ism" — Alcoholism. Workaholism. Religiousholism. Basically this means having a primary relationship with something other than your partner. What gets your time, your attention, your energy, your passion is your "ism" and not your partner. If you'd rather be at the office or bar or church or wherever than be at home, it's an avoidance technique. One of my clients put it this way, "If I stay away, I can't get beat up. Or at least it doesn't last as long."

Any addictions — This is similar to #1 above. Drug addiction (even pot). Food addiction. Exercise addiction. Sex addiction (which includes but is not limited to going to topless bars, going to prostitutes, downloading porn from the internet, etc.). Television. Music. Sports (which includes but is not limited to playing sports, watching sports, coaching sports, playing fantasy sports, reading about sports, and memorizing sports' statistics). Internet addiction. Gambling. Really just about any healthy behavior can cross the line into addiction where it starts to take over more and more of your time, energy, and thought process. Usually it happens slowly, without your knowing it. I know a man whose addiction is researching his genealogy. He's obsessed with it. The planning of his day revolves around how he can most quickly get done with his work so that he can get to what he really wants to do — his research. In the meantime, his wife is languishing — and hurricaning.

Infidelity — Having an affair or multiple affairs. Having an emotional affair. This is an avoidance technique. Men often describe their affairs to me as, "A little oasis. A place where I'm appreciated and valued." Not having the tools to create intimacy in their primary relationship, men often substitute "pseudo intimacy" as a way to feel some sense of personal power.

Lying — Men often learn that one way to avoid the hurricane for the moment is just to lie. "Yes, I did the taxes." "Of course I called him back." "No, I didn't forget to (fill in the blank) — I did it this morning (which means I need to remember to do that first thing tomorrow so I don't get caught)." Another way of lying is just leaving out information. "I didn't tell you because I knew you'd get upset." "I didn't tell you because I knew it would hurt you." "I was going to tell you after I got it all cleared up." "I wasn't keeping it from you — I was planning on telling you, but I haven't had a chance yet." This, too, is an avoidance technique. The truth of the matter is, information is withheld on purpose to avoid getting beat up by the hurricane.

An underground life — Lots of silence here. Not much conversation. Secret thoughts. Secret behaviors. No real accounting of your time to your partner. I had one client who traveled a lot. He had a wife and son in Texas as well as a girlfriend and two daughters in Ohio, not to mention his girlfriend in California. When it got too overwhelming with one woman he scheduled a business trip to hook up with another. On the surface this man might look like he had the world on a string. But believe me, underneath he described feeling so out of control, feeling no authentic power, and that he was constantly on the run. Scared. Powerless. Lonely. He said, "Instead of having one woman who beats me up, I have three who do."

Checking out — Pulling the plug. Just not trying. Not putting any effort into making things better in your relationship. Being so busy or preoccupied that you don't respond to your wife's pain.

Running away — Literally getting up and leaving the room whenever your partner wants to talk. Refusing to engage in any conversation about any potentially controversial subject (which includes just about every topic). Not coming home right after work but maybe stopping for a movie first. Going to bed at 8:00 each night. Taking an assignment out of town for a year or two. Avoidance.

The second coping mechanism employed to deal with the hurricane is fight. I've had several clients tell me over the years that they identify with the bullfrog. When the hurricane starts, they just puff and puff and puff themselves up to twice their normal size to scare off the attacker. They have learned that this works to keep them safe. It is, however, once again not authentic power. It's an act. It's an effective act, but an act nonetheless. What does it look like? Here are a few common examples, but again, not all the mutations this coping mechanism takes.

Fight

Raging — Often when the hurricane starts, the emotionally unavailable man will hurricane back. Louder. That is, it is *in reaction to* his wife's behavior. She screams, she yells, she throws things, she curses. So he screams, he yells, he throws things, he curses right back. Louder. Bigger. All puffed up until she shuts up.

Battering — This is an escalation of #1. Men hit their wives/girlfriends when they feel powerless or emasculated. Of course, there are other causes of battering but going from raging to physical abuse is a small step for some men when they feel victimized by their partner. Having no authentic power, they opt for "pseudo power."

Condescension — One attack that men use when their wives begin to cry or show hurt feelings is to put the partner down. Make fun of her. Accuse her of going into her "crying act." They might say something like, "Oh, yeah! Here we go again! Turn on the tears! Turn on the crying machine!" They give the impression that having all those emotions is inferior, stupid, not effective, certainly a manipulation, an irritation, and of course, nothing to be taken seriously. They may smile at their partner's tears or even laugh.

A variation on this theme is making your partner crazy: "You're crazy. I mean there's something wrong with you. You're not normal. You're nuts! What a stupid thing to say. I'm telling you, you are not dealing with a full deck. Look at yourself! You're a mess."

And then, of course, blaming your partner: "No wonder I don't come home (or I drink or I eat or whatever). Who would want to come home to this?"

All of these approaches are part of the "fight" response.

Being loud, being irritated, being unpleasant, being rude, being accusatory — The emotionally unavailable man may not go so far as raging to shut up his partner, he may just fight by being hard to communicate with: "What did you *want* me to do? Oh, yeah, YOU got all the answers! You don't know what you're talking about. I'm sick of listening to all this crap! You make me sick." Etc.

Passive aggressiveness/crazy communication — Some men fight more subtly. Less openly. Passive aggressiveness is anger that has gone underground and comes out sideways. There are thousands of ways to be passive aggressive. One might be late coming home. Without calling. One might make promises and then "forget" to keep them. Special days slip by without any acknowledgment. Unilateral decisions are made: "Oh, I didn't think you'd want to be *consulted* about my buying a motorcycle." The partner is excluded, left out: "I'm sure I told you the company party was tonight (15 minutes before the husband is planning to walk out the door)."

And then there's crazy communication. There are many variations to this theme as well. Not answering the question asked. Staring blankly at your partner in silence. Not responding at all to a question. Focusing on a tangent instead of a high priority. The example I use with my clients is the wife screams, "Oh, my God! There's a Bengal tiger chasing us!" And the husband responds with, "Bengal tiger? What makes you think that's a Bengal tiger? I think it's a Siberian tiger. Didn't you pay attention in geography class when you were in high school? I am SURE that's a Siberian tiger!" Crazy communication is really not communication at all. It's a subtle way of fighting.

All of these behaviors are attack modes. Fight. All are attempts to shut the hurricane up and to not be victimized by it. And they may serve this purpose well. However, all are not effective ways of connecting with your partner. All are not effective ways to obtain long term gratification. Inner peace. Love. Freedom. And power. All are not ways of being emotionally available. All are not ways to achieve — AND THIS IS THE GOAL — authentic power, freedom, choice, and true happiness.

So, whether a man uses avoidance or fight as his coping mechanism — or a combination of both — he is still unable to claim his lost self, his emotions, his true power. Therefore, he is still at a disadvantage, I believe, in intimate relationships. He is still *reacting to* his partner. Not *responding* to, but *reacting* to. That is, his behavior is not determined by himself, but by his partner's behavior.

Reacting

Consider a 17 year old high school senior. He has been told since he could walk that he would be a Texas Aggie some day. He wore Texas A&M T-shirts since he was 2 days old. His father was an Aggie, his mother was an inferior Texas Longhorn from the University of Texas in Austin. By golly, HE was going to be an Aggie. So, at 17, making his college choice, this boy could say, "Okay, I guess I'm going to A&M. There's no way my father will let me go anywhere else.

But I like the school. I think it'll be great." Or he could say, "F- You! I'm NOT going to A&M. In fact there is nothing you could do to EVER make me go to A&M! That's the LAST school I'll ever go to!" Now both of these "choices" he's making are not really choices. They are both *reactions*. Both of these "choices" are "pseudo choices." The boy thinks he is making an independent choice, but in reality he is deciding something based on his father's wishes. Real power comes from real choice. Real choice in this situation would be if the boy could extricate his father's wishes from the equation (which would be almost impossible to do at age 17 with a power parent) and say to himself, "Do I even like A&M? Is it the best choice for my major?" If he wants to be a veterinarian, A&M is a great choice. If he wants to be a professional musician, forget A&M. It's not a great choice. Real choice, therefore, is picking a school based on the boy's needs and wants and not on his father's wishes. It is very different than reactionary fight or flight.

Reactionary fight or flight, I hate to tell you, just fuels the hurricane.

Chapter 4

The Hurricane from the Woman's Point of View

First of all, little girls are not, in general, encouraged to cut off from their feelings. They are allowed to cry. In fact, they are usually comforted when they cry. Nurtured. They are allowed to be scared. A little 5-year-old girl who's afraid of the dark is held, reassured, given a teddy bear to sleep with. A little 5-year-old boy so often hears, "Big boys aren't afraid of the dark," or "You're not afraid. You're a big boy," and sometimes, "Stop crying! Don't be a sissy." What different worlds these two children live in!

So what happens when our children grow up? We have men who don't have their emotions available to them anymore and we have women who do. Then, we put these two together and watch the battle begin — all the while puzzling, "I wonder why they're not getting along . . ."

Why? Because we are setting up little boys to be emotionally unavailable men and, at the same time, setting up little girls to be emotionally unhappy women. How? By teaching our little girls that they are princesses. Special. And that someday their prince will come. Not only will their prince come, but he will be strong, smart, romantic and will take care of their every princess need and desire. Little princesses are taught the fantasy that they will be whisked away by the man of their dreams. That man being, of course, someone who will meet all of her needs — especially emotionally. That man will have undying love and devotion for the princess. And, by the way, no needs of his own.

Please, gag me. I can't stand that this myth is still perpetuated on our little girls in the 21st century. BUT IT IS. They are taught to be pretty, polite, sexy, and manipulative so that one day they'll be able to capture the heart of their prince, get married, and live happily ever after. It's the Cinderella Complex, and it is alive and well today.

When I was a senior in high school we were given our class rank. Well, I had always made straight A's, but still I was shocked to find out that I was ranked 1st out of my 625 classmates. I remember feeling somewhat embarrassed by it and scared that people would find out (Duh! Of course they would!). I felt shame, though. Why? Because my mother had taught me to hide my calculus grades, to hide my highest score on the test grades, and to *especially* not let the boys see it. My mother, coming from the old school, told me, "Boys are threatened by smart girls," and that "boys don't want to date anyone smarter than them." So where did that leave me ranked first? An old maid. Dateless. My fear was I'd be undatable, unloved, and my prince wouldn't come. Now this all may seem *ridiculous* from a male point of view — and it is certainly ridiculous from my point of view today (as well as my mother's) — but I am telling you, this is what little girls are taught.

My mother's solution to my problem of brains was to "not let on" and to always make the man feel smarter. I was also told, by both my mother and father, that girls don't need to go to college. When I said I wanted to go to college, my mother suggested I go to an Ivy League school for one year so I could get my MRS Degree. True story.

And it's still being taught to our little girls today. Believe me. I hear it in my office everyday. I hear it from my 8-year-old son's female third grade classmates. If you have a daughter, is she a princess?

What a set up for little girls! What a set up to be taught a wonderful prince will come along and meet all your emotional needs while at the same time we are teaching our little boys not to feel. To be tough. To cut off from their emotional selves. The Catch 22, of course, is that if a person is not in touch with his emotional self, he cannot meet emotional needs of others. Those tools are not available.

That is a very important sentence: If a person is not in touch with his emotional self, he cannot meet emotional needs of others.

And women have emotional needs. (As, of course, do men.)

So here we have this little princess who has grown up and married her prince only to find out HE can't meet her emotional needs! Disillusionment sets in for her. This is not how the story goes. What about the happily ever after part? She begins to feel angry, cheated, ripped off. The storm begins to brew. The wife begins to criticize her partner or cry or hurt or yell. She may not even know why she's so unhappy — she may be totally unaware of how much she has been culturally lied to and set up — but she knows she's unhappy and it's YOUR FAULT. You are the one who is not keeping up your end of the bargain — you know, the prince part where you meet her every princess need and desire. The storm gains strength. At this point she may begin to think she married the wrong person. You, after all, are not her prince.

Now, if the man has been taught to cut off from his emotional self as a child, which is likely, he is bewildered. He doesn't even know what she's talking about. He doesn't get it. (If this describes you, keep reading.) He may stand there like a deer in the middle of the road staring at the oncoming headlights, paralyzed with fear and a feeling of inadequacy. He may try to comfort his wife or girlfriend but remember, if his emotional self is not available to him, he cannot meet the emotional needs of his partner. Her emotions don't make sense to him. He's in a no win situation.

So the winds gain strength and whirl into a tropical storm. The wife feels SO frustrated. Now, depending on whether the emotionally unavailable man uses fight or flight as his coping mechanism, the woman may either feel like the victim or become the victimizer. The Poor Pitiful Me or the Big Bad Wolf. The relentless, pounding hurricane has arrived.

This leaves the woman not only feeling disillusioned, lied to, ripped off, unheard, frustrated to the max, but also misunderstood. She feels she is not the Poor Pitiful Me or the Big Bad Wolf and doesn't want to be pigeonholed into these one dimensional roles. She especially resents the bad guy role. She is only yelling to try to get the story to come out like it's supposed to. She hates being treated like something big and bad because she's still really just that little girl wanting to be taken care of by her partner. THAT'S how the story GOES. This makes her feel even more angry, ripped off, lonely, and frustrated. She cannot get her partner to understand. She cannot get him to fix it and be her prince and meet all her princess needs and desires.

Of course she can't! Because her partner doesn't get it. And her partner can't get it without his emotional self which he left behind in his past when he was 8 years old. It's a vicious cycle that cannot be resolved without the male reclaiming his emotions.

So how does he do that?

Chapter 5

Facing the Storm

By facing the storm.

Now this might sound like a crazy idea to you since you've spent a lifetime trying to get away from the storm, but it *is* a necessary step to claim your authentic power and your emotional self.

To face the storm you must learn to *respond* to it rather than *react* to it. To do this, you are going to need five tools. The first three are developed internally. The last two are developed experientially. That is, through the practice and experience of using these two tools, you will develop them. The five tools you will need are:

1. The realization that you are not a victim

2. The realization that you have needs, too

3. The realization that your decisions and behaviors have been fear-based

4. You'll need a voice

5. You'll need boundaries

Tool #1 In Facing the Storm:
The Realization That You Are Not a Victim

Let me make it clear that I believe that as a child you were a victim. You did not have choice. Also as a child you got your subconscious programming about how to be in the world and how the world works. We all did. You didn't have a choice about that either. Now, though, as an adult, you do have choice. And you can choose not to be a victim. How do you do that? By examining your subconscious childhood programming.

You see, our brains and psyches are just like huge computers. We are programmed as children to act and feel a certain way toward certain stimuli. Those programs keep running without interruption until what I call our moment of awakening. Before that, we're all just asleep letting our programming run our lives — without even being aware of it. For example, let's say you were the firstborn child of two parents who both worked and were gone a lot. You were given the unspoken role of caretaker for your three younger siblings. You were the one who got them ready for school in the mornings and had to be home when they got off the school bus. You were who they came to with their problems. You were the fixer. As an adult you may continue in the caretaker/fixer role by dating women who are somehow "broken" or "childlike" and need your help. This is subconscious programming.

This tool, the realization that you are not a victim, is the interruption needed to wake up and take charge of your computer/your subconscious programming.

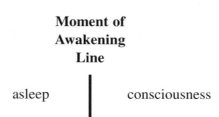

**Moment of
Awakening
Line**

asleep | consciousness

Some people do this crossover from asleep to awake/consciousness quickly – an "Aha!" moment — and some people do this gradually. Either way, *awakening* is necessary. Why? Because a lot of the programming you got as a child was inaccurate. They lied to you. They gave you wrong data. It really wasn't *your* job to take care of your three younger siblings: it was your *parents'* job. This is the moment for you to realize that you have been operating your computer with incorrect information. So, of course, you cannot draw correct conclusions. This is not your fault. You are not to blame. You were given incorrect data and didn't know it.

It reminds me of proving theorems in geometry class. If any of the data in your proof is inaccurate, you get the wrong answer. So it is in your brain. And a lot of the data you have been operating with is inaccurate.

I tell my clients — and they often think this is very radical — that I don't hold them — or you — responsible for any of their/your behavior until they/you have crossed the awakening line. Before that you are simply acting out of your subconscious programming. Unaware. Unaware even of why you are doing what you're doing. I have had so many men tell me how puzzled they are at their self-destructive behaviors. They say, "I KNOW what I'm doing is wrong, not in my best interest (having an affair, not being financially responsible, lying, not applying themselves at work, etc.), but I keep doing it. I don't understand *why*." Why? Programming. You have been programmed as a child to behave the way you are behaving. You have been programmed to act out of a child ego state particularly in relationships where emotions are involved. To fight or flight. To avoid.

Remember, emotionally unavailable men were taught as children that emotions are not safe or desirable. Emotionally unavailable men were taught as children that there is NO WAY to negotiate the storm. Emotionally unavailable men were taught that they don't have what it takes to make things different. This is part of the erroneous data that was fed into your computer and that you are still operating under. No wonder you have trouble in intimate relationships!

Two Ego States

Basically as human beings we all have two ego states: the child ego state and the adult ego state. We — all of us — operate in the child ego state before crossing the line of awakening. I say all of us because I want you to know that you are NORMAL. No one — and let me make it clear, NO ONE — escapes subconscious programming in his childhood. It's the same with death — no one gets out of it. And you are no exception to those rules. You got subconscious programming as a child: you're going to die someday, too. YOU ARE NORMAL. You are not flawed. You are HUMAN. ALL OF US operate in our child ego state until the moment of awakening when we realize we have choice. We are only able to operate in our adult ego state once we have crossed the line of awakening. No matter how old you are. And may it be duly noted, too, that some people never cross that line of awakening and they live their entire lives operating out of their child ego state and programming. They spend their entire lives asleep. Let's not let you be one of those people. Why? Because when you operate from a child ego state, you do not have your personal authentic power, and you cannot develop into all that you can be. Ever. No way. You are simply acting from your programming.

The goal is to cross the line into awakening and realize when you are in your child ego state and when you are not. After that, it is important to *choose* to operate from your adult ego state. Here are some differences of the two ego states so that you can begin to identify when you are in each state:

Moment of Awakening Line

CHILD EGO STATE	ADULT EGO STATE
victim stance	non-victim stance:
	I am not a victim
often feels powerless	feels powerful
no choice: "I have to"	ALWAYS choice
reactive	proactive
not responsible	always responsible
it's not my fault	I have a part and I own it
defensive	feels no need to defend

So, the first tool you need to face the storm is the realization that you are not a victim. You have been operating from your child ego state and in a victim stance because that is HOW YOU WERE PRO-GRAMMED. It's what you were taught. But, now that you are an adult, you have a choice as to whether or not to continue to allow your child programming to run your life. As an adult you have CHOICE as to whether or not you want to stay in your child ego state and childhood programming. It's sort of like letting a 5-year-old drive your car. Your emotional car. Do you really want to do that? Because that's what you're doing. Not on purpose, not out of awareness, but because that is how you were programmed to operate. It's time to change that.

Often, when I'm working with a man and we talk about the two ego states, I run into resistance right now. We might go through several sessions of his explaining certain circumstances and what his behavior was in those circumstances. And time and time again I can ask, 'Was your behavior adult or child?' and he can clearly identify it as child. But he keeps being in child. Over and over and over again. For example, a client might explain to me his wife's crazy, irrational, outrageous raging at him about not taking out the garbage — one more time. When I ask him what he did in response to this rage, he'll say, "I just took it. Sucked it up and then took out the garbage." I ask adult or child behavior? He can clearly see it as child. Then I ask him, why are you choosing child?

And I ask you that question, too. Why are you choosing child? The answers I get most frequently are:

- It's easier — which is child.

- I don't know what else to do — which is child.

- It won't do any good anyway — which is child (Remember the erroneous data you were taught? You're still believing it).

- I guess I don't want to grow up — it's scary — which is child.

- It's too much responsibility to be an adult (translation from that inaccurate data: I don't have what it takes) — which is child. Be gentle with yourself. You've been given erroneous data to run. You've been running it for years, for so long that you believe the data to be true. And I'm here to tell you, IT IS NOT TRUE. You are capable. You are competent. You *can* figure out what your choices are and make good decisions. You *can* influence the storm. You can STOP the storm. You can be a full-fledged adult and have your personal power at ALL times. You are capable of handling the responsibility of adult. Adult just means that I am response-able: able to respond (rather than re-act). I have my personal power and authority at all times and I have choice at all times. It means you have choice about whether or not your erroneous data is going to be left in charge.

In fact, as an adult you *always* have choice. ALWAYS. As a child you didn't. When you fully embrace this concept of choice then you will have crossed the line of awakening. You are no longer a victim. You can no longer let your programming run you without conscious thought about it and making a choice about it.

If there were an alternative title to this book, it would be:

You Are Not a Victim: You Have Choice.

I was in a support group in my early 20's and I was lamenting how my boyfriend had done this and that and had been so mean in saying this and then that, when suddenly one of the other women in the group screamed at me, "YOU ARE NOT A F—ING VICTIM!" Well, I was stunned. She clearly didn't understand that I *was* indeed a victim. I lowered my head and cried — and never went back to the group. But, I tell you this, that was my moment of awakening. I thought about what she said over and over and over again. For days, for weeks. Then I finally got it, "She's right. I am NOT a victim. I have choices, and I'm not exercising them." That day, that woman, changed my life forever. I have no idea who she was. Still, I know she was one of the messengers in my life sent to get me to "get it." To wake up.

And that's what I'm saying to you. Wake up. You are not a victim! You have choice. ALWAYS.

You have choice whether or not to believe someone's assessment of you. You have choice about how you respond to something or someone. You have choice whether to stand there and get emotionally battered. You have choice about your attitude, about how big or small you make something, about how good or bad you make it. You have choice about making the cup half empty or half full. You have choice about your relationship. If it's bad you have three choices: make it worse (end it), keep it the same (stay in victim and act out), or make it better (get in your adult ego state and change things). YOU get to decide. Not your wife.

You have choice even when people tell you that you don't have choice. Even when people insist you don't have choice, you do. They're lying to you. You always have choice. When you fully embrace this concept of choice you can never be a victim to anyone again. Unless you *choose* that. Then, of course, you are not really a victim since you are consciously choosing a victim stance. You are still responsible for your choice. With choice you become your own authority. You do not give your authority away to ANYONE. EVER. Only you are in charge of your thoughts, feelings and behaviors. No one can MAKE you do anything. Hey, this is America. You get to choose your experience.

When I was pregnant with my second son I was over 35. When I went for a monthly checkup my gynecologist, whom I love and respect, wrote out an order for me to have an amniocentesis. I said to him, "Oh, I'm not doing that," to which he replied, "Oh, yes you are. I'm your doctor, you're over 35, you're having an amnio." Now, there was no reason to power struggle with him. I was quite clear this is America, and I wasn't having an amnio, so I said, "Actually I'm quite clear I'm not." You see I had already thought it through, looked at my choices, and decided against an amnio. My husband and I had faced infertility issues for years and I had finally gotten pregnant. I knew an amnio was used to tell the health of the baby (including whether or not it had Down's Syndrome) and could be used to assess whether or not the mother wanted to have an abortion. I also knew I would not have an abortion. It did not matter to my husband and me if this baby were a special needs child or not — we wanted the baby. I further knew that, though remote, amnios could cause miscarriages. I wasn't willing to take that chance.

My doctor then called his nurse into our room and said, "Let me get this straight. I am your doctor and I am telling you to have an amniocentesis, and you are refusing to have this test run. Is that correct?" and I said, "Yes." "So, you are clearly going against my medical advice — is that right?" Again, I said, "Yes." To which he replied, "Good for you. Note it on her chart, please."

You see, he was just covering HIS rear. People are often insistent that you do something because it's good for THEM — not you. Therefore you must hold onto your personal power and your choice. In this case, my doctor then told me about one of his patients who, after thirteen years of infertility problems, had an amnio and ended up miscarrying because of it. Wow. I'm glad I held onto my authority and didn't listen to his.

NEVER give up your power or authority to ANYONE. You always have choice. I don't care if you just got fired from your lifetime job, you still have choice. How you are going to respond to it is up to you: if you have been wronged and need to start gathering evidence for a court case, if you are going to embrace joyfully the end of one chapter of your life to open a new one, if you are going to figure out why this happened to you at this point in your life or whatever. The point is, you still have choice. I remember working with a woman who was raped by her estranged husband and became pregnant. She was deep in grief about having no choice but to have an abortion. I said, "Well, you do have some other options, you know." She insisted she didn't so I spelled out the obvious: keep the pregnancy and the child or keep the pregnancy and give the child up for adoption. To which she responded, "Sure I have choices, but they're all shitty choices!" And you know, sometimes that is true: they are all shitty choices. So I say pick the least shitty, and then change your attitude about it. Remember, you are not a victim. You get to decide what your experience will be like. Several years later this client called to thank me for insisting that she look at all of her choices and then to take ownership of the one she picked. Otherwise, she would have felt victimized for years. As it turned out, she did choose to keep the pregnancy and to keep the baby.

The father had given up his parental rights and she was remarrying a wonderful man. A happy ending. But I tell you it was only happy because she got out of her victim stance and made CONSCIOUS choices. She said it was her moment of crossing the line of awakening.

In Victor Frankl's incredible book, *Man's Search for Meaning*, he speaks about his concentration camp experiences. He speaks of the power of choice that we all have.

> Do the prisoners' reactions to the singular world of the concentration camp prove that man cannot escape the influences of his surroundings? Does man have no choice of action in such circumstances? We can answer these questions from experience as well as on principle. The experiences of camp life show that man does have choice of action. There were enough examples, often of a heroic nature, which proved that apathy could be overcome, irritability suppressed. Man *can* preserve a vestige of spiritual freedom, of independence of mind, even in such terrible conditions of psychic and physical stress.

> We who lived in concentration camps can remember the men who walked through the huts comforting others, giving away their last piece of bread. They may have been few in number, but they offer sufficient proof that everything can be taken from a man but one thing: the last of the human freedoms — to choose one's attitude in any given set of circumstances, to choose one's own way. (page 86)

Even under the most horrific circumstances, Frankl reminds us that we all have choice. Everyday, at every juncture. Choice about our thoughts, our feelings, our attitudes.

You are not a victim. You can hold onto your authority and power even in the face of the storm. This is tool #1. This is the mantra you must repeat over and over and over to yourself:

I Am Not a Victim. I Have Choice.

Tool #2 In Facing the Storm:
The Realization That You Have Needs, Too

So many little boys are taught not to have needs — to repress this longing until they can't feel it pushing anymore. They are also taught that having needs means they are weak. If you were taught those things, you were lied to. Having needs is not weak. It is normal. You are not from some alien planet made up of alien matter. You are from this planet reading this book which makes you human. Humans have needs. Period. All of us. Try going a day or two without oxygen if you think you don't. If you think you're different. You're not. You're one of us. When your skin gets cut, you bleed. You are part of the human race designed and constructed to have physical and emotional needs.

So, bear with me and accept that premise for a moment. The premise that you are normal, you are not different from the rest of the human race, and so you have physical and emotional needs. The physical needs I want you to acknowledge to yourself are the need for touch and the need for safety. The emotional needs I want you to acknowledge to yourself are the need for safety, the need for power, and the need for acceptance/love.

Touch

Of course, your physical needs include the need for oxygen, food, water, shelter from the elements, the basics. But for our purposes I want you to focus in on accepting that you have a need to be touched. This does not make you weak or flawed; it makes you human. If you ever took Psychology 101 you probably learned of the rhesus monkey experiments by Harry Harlow. These baby monkeys were "fed" by either a wooden monkey covered by soft cloth or a wire mesh monkey. Within a matter of DAYS the babies fed by the wire monkeys became depressed and withdrawn and began to act neurotic. They would curl themselves into a fetal position and rock themselves. Eventually, they became despondent, lost all interest in life, stopped feeding — and DIED. It was difficult for them to make it past their first five days.

Now we've never done that experiment on humans — for obvious reasons — but if it were possible, I believe we'd get the same results. People need (not want), NEED physical contact. They thrive when they get it, and wither when they don't. You — because you are in this people category — are no exception. You have a need to be touched. Yes, you can get this need somewhat satisfied by animals — by holding them, letting them sit on your feet, petting them, etc., but so much more so with humans. You have a need to be held and hugged and caressed and touched. By an adult. I will go so far as to say and made love to. Now you won't die like the monkeys if you are not made love to, but I believe it will restrict your ability to thrive. Therefore, if you are in a relationship where you are not touched, held, hugged, caressed, and made love to, that is not okay. That needs to change. Your physical needs — and your partner's — are not getting met.

Safety

Another physical need that you have is also an emotional need. That is the need for safety. In fact, I believe it is one of the greatest — if not THE greatest — need we have. That's why you have developed all these creative and ingenious coping mechanisms to protect yourself. You were programmed as a child that emotions were not safe and that as a boy you were not supposed to even have them. And therefore, you have developed lots of subconscious coping mechanisms to keep yourself safe from them. In fact, that has been your goal in life: do whatever it is you need to do to keep yourself safe. Even if it means disappearing. Even if it means abandoning yourself. That's the program you've been running in your computer since you were a little boy. This book is about changing that program.

But not changing your need for safety. That is NORMAL. You are NORMAL. Needing safety, both physically and emotionally, is NORMAL. Unfortunately, because you have been programmed with erroneous data, you are set up to think you can only be safe when you are not truly connected. Not truly connected to your emotional self, not truly connected to your partner's emotional self. This is sort of a "pseudo safety." True safety comes from having your authentic power, never giving up your authority, always having choice, and having your full self available to you — including your emotional self. True safety is when you can fully connect with someone — your partner — and not give ANY of yourself away. I liken good relationships to sending a fax. You send your partner a fax and you get to keep the original. NEVER do you give yourself or your power away.

Power

Which brings us to another need: the need for power. We all have the need to feel powerful. To feel valuable. To feel like we have worth. To feel like we can influence our world. That we can make a difference. That our words can have an impact.

When I teach parenting classes I teach this concept about children. They have so little power that it is frustrating for them. If we strip children of the small amount of power they do have, we change them forever. In a bad way. I tell parents: give your children choice. I don't care if it's asking your 3 year old if he wants to wear a green shirt or a blue shirt, let him pick. With a 6 year old, tell him he can either pick up his room or the game room. Let him choose. With a 12 year old, whether he takes a shower in the morning or night, whether he shoots hoops for an hour before or after homework, whether he wants long hair or short hair. I'm not talking about giving children carte blanche. Letting them decide *everything*. They are not developmentally equipped to make responsible choices about everything. I'm talking about giving them room to make choices, and have a sense of personal power, whenever it is possible and appropriate. You will find you have a less angry child. Less confrontational. Less resistant. More cooperative. Why? Because they are able to feel some sense of personal power. They need to learn that they are not going to win all the battles they face, but that they can win some of them.

If a child — a man, a country — believes he can win NONE of the battles, which often happens when being raised by a power parent, he will become angry and act out, or become angry/afraid and go underground.

It's the same with adults. We all need a sense of personal power. We need to know we are heard and can have some impact on any given situation. We do not have a need, I believe, to have ALL the impact in ALL situations. It's my observation that people seem to be able to live in balance and at peace with having SOME of the impact in SOME situations. We don't have to win all of the time, but we do have to win some of the time.

An Example

My 15-year-old son plays a card game at school with his buddies every lunch hour called VC. It's a complex game with lots of strategy involved. About once a week or so he'll ask me to play a few games with him. And I do. And I lose. Then he begs me to play a few more. Finally, after weeks of this pattern, I said to him, "And what's the fun part of this game?" You see, he was having a blast. Winning and winning and winning. I was not. He spent hours a week practicing this game; I felt lucky to even remember the rules. It wasn't fun for me to ALWAYS lose. He lost sometimes — at school — but could pretty much count on creaming me.

So, at this point, I need you to acknowledge to yourself your need for a sense of personal power and to furthermore understand that, if this need is not getting met, it leads to all kinds of acting out. What kind of acting out do you do? Is it overt (out in the open) or covert (hidden)? Whatever your style, it would be good to start to look for it. Start to see it; be aware of it. You don't have to change it at all just yet. Right now the only thing you have to do is become conscious of it. So many partners do not understand that when they hurricane, make unilateral decisions, emasculate, and practice character assassination, that this may strip the partner's power away on the surface, but it does NOT— CANNOT — take away the person's need for power. It can sublimate the need — but not take it away. Because it's innate. That need will come out somewhere — it doesn't go away. It may *look* like it goes away — he/she may capitulate — but in the depth of a person's soul, it's still there.

You must come to understand this about yourself so that you can begin to make sense out of your behavior and even begin to forgive yourself. Be kind to yourself. Also, you must acknowledge your need for a sense of power so that you can begin to say no when the answer is no and yes when the answer is yes. If you are saying yes when the answer is no, you are giving away your personal power. But not your *need* for personal power. It's innate. In born. We need it like we need oxygen. So when you give your personal power away, it's only a matter of time until there is a repercussion of that. A repercussion that comes out directly or comes out sideways. You cannot continually give in, give your personal power away, without some kind of consequence (i.e., disconnecting from your partner, raging, lying, cheating, developing an "ism", being passive aggressive, etc.).

But back to tool one: You are not a victim here. You do have choice. You have a choice as to whether or not you give your power away. NO ONE can take it from you. You have to give it.

Choice

So, I want you to begin to think in terms of choice. I want you to begin to think in terms of you have a choice of whether or not to give your personal power away. I know this concept of 'always having a choice' is often difficult to understand — or even to believe — if you've been raised by a power parent and/or are married to a power spouse. This is because as a child you had no choice. But now, as an adult, I'm telling you, you do.

I want you to think about your having a NEED for power (like oxygen) and your willingness to give it away. This will guarantee an undesirable long term consequence. So, do you really want to choose to give it away?

Why choose that? It's going to come back and bite you. Guaranteed. It WILL work against you if you give your power away and get in the victim stance. At the very least it will prevent you from getting the benefits of connecting with a partner on a deep level. Think about it. Stop giving your power away.

One last thing: You may find this hard to believe, but your partner does not *want* your power. She wants you to know, to lead, to have an answer. She wants you to be self-defined and proactive. I cannot tell you how many couples I've worked with, where the wife clearly had the power in the relationship, and her exclamation was, "I don't want his power!" And further, "I don't want another child to raise!" She wants you to have your power and to act on the world as an adult *even when she does or says things to the contrary*. (See the women's side of the book, Chapter 5). So, for your sake and hers, hold onto your power.

Love and Acceptance

The fourth need that you have — because you're normal — is a need for love and acceptance. Sometimes I am in awe of this when I see it in my husband. When I really see it and don't just see him as this strong person there to meet *my* needs, but as a person with needs of his own. For tenderness, for kindness, for grace, for acceptance. We all need to belong. We all need to know we are good enough. Lovable. You are no different. I had a saying on my refrigerator for years, "Every baby is born with the need to be loved — and never outgrows it." You are no different. There is nothing wrong with longing for acceptance and love. That is NORMAL. That is why we keep remarrying. Yes, the divorce rate is still about 50 percent, but even after one or two or three bad marriages, we fall in love and marry again. Still hoping. Still longing to get that need for love and acceptance met. There's nothing weak about that. It's normal.

To get this need met, you have to get on your side as far as love and acceptance goes. Yes, it's ideal to get this need met by your partner, but you also must take some responsibility here. First, let's look at where you stand.

You can get a good view of this by doing an exercise called a voice dialogue. It is one of the few exercises I ask you to do in this book. There aren't a lot of them because I'm not into exercises. This one, however, is important. Get out a pen and paper and a watch. This exercise will take six minutes of your life — and could well change your life in a dramatic way. Don't skip this one.

Voice Dialogue

We all have many voices in our head that talk to us. When the alarm goes off in the morning one voice says, "Ugh." Another might say, "Okay, get up." Another, "No, one more snooze." Yet another might say, "What day is it? Oh —expletive — it's Monday and I've got that early plane to catch!" This is NORMAL.

Now I want you to try to isolate two of these voices and write down on your piece of paper what they say to you. First of all, I want you to write down things that your critical voice says to you. Not what it theoretically says to you, but what you actually tell yourself. Here are some examples of the critical voice:

- I'm so stupid (or fat, or a nerd, or worthless, or a screw-up, or an idiot, dumb, incompetent, ridiculous, ugly, etc.)
- You can't do that. No way. Are you crazy?
- God, you're getting fat (or old or bald, etc.).
- What were you thinking? You're such a screw up.
- Well, it figures. Tom got the promotion. Not me. One more time. I'm a worthless piece of sh—, that's why.
- I'm not a good father (husband, partner, person, etc.).

What do you tell yourself? Write for three minutes everything your critical voice says to you. If you don't want to write it, just say it out loud or in your head. Write it if you can — it's more effective.

Next, I want you to write down everything your affirming (supportive) voice says to you. What do you say NICE to yourself?

Examples of the affirming voice are:

- I'm smart (good-looking, a nice person, handy, friendly, compassionate, honest, etc.)
- I can do that. I can figure it out.
- I'm a good father (husband, worker, partner, etc.)
- I'm kind.
- I'm resourceful.
- I'm funny.

Again, don't write down things you COULD say to yourself. Write down what you DO say to yourself. And if your critical voice interrupts you, write that on your critical sheet. For example, if your affirming voice says, "I'm a nice person," and then your critical voice chimes in, "Well, sometimes," that goes on your critical list. Write for three minutes.

Who's In Charge?

That's the end of the exercise. What did you find out? Who's in charge — your critical voice or your affirming voice? Also, if your critical voice is your mother or father speaking, who is it? Often, we have internalized one of our parent's critical voices so much so that we don't need our parent to criticize us anymore — we do it ourselves! Your parent may be dead and gone — and still in charge. Still criticizing you through your own critical voice.

So, if you found out that your critical voice outweighs your affirming voice, that's not okay. That needs to change. We want your affirming voice to be loud and strong in your head and your critical voice to seldom pipe up. That way you can begin to love and accept yourself at a deeper level. With personal love and acceptance you can come to expect love and acceptance from others in your life, as well.

In my own recovery, I started to increase my internal affirming voice by saying, "I am a good person." It was the only positive thing I could believe about myself at the time — and really only half believe. You need to find a positive statement about yourself that you can believe and begin to say to yourself. Like a mantra. Fifty times a day — everyday. You want to change? You've got to change what you tell yourself. Period. There's no other way to get there. You MUST change your internal dialogue. Other statements my clients have used are:

- I am enough.
- I am good enough.
- I am lovable.
- I have value.
- I am a good person and deserve good treatment.

Try these on. Pick one of these or any other statement that works for you. You don't have to totally believe it when you begin the process, but you do have to say it to yourself over and over again. Also, when your critical voice pipes up to discount your positive affirmation (it will), silence it. Tell it to shut up. Tell it it's fired. Tell it you're not listening to it anymore. Tell it you don't believe it anymore. The point is to decrease the power of your critical voice and to increase the power of your affirming/supportive voice. This may seem Mickey Mouse or even weird. Try not to let that get in your way and do it anyway. Why? Because it works. It is necessary to reprogram your "computer" because you've been running on some very self-destructive data. Take that data out — put new data in. Think of it this way: all of your best decisions thus far have brought you to where you are. If you want to reap more of the benefits of life, you have to make some different decisions. This is one of them. Decide to silence your critical voice and bulk up your affirming one. It will make a difference in your life. As you love yourself more, you will come to tolerate nothing less than that from your partner. You're a good person. You deserve good treatment.

So to review:

- You are not a victim. Stop acting like one.
- You have needs, too, and deserve to get those met.

Tool #3 In Facing the Storm:
The Realization That Your Decisions
and Behaviors Are Fear-Based

This is the third tool you'll need to face the storm and hold onto your personal power. As children we know instinctively that if we are not cared for by an adult, we will die. And this is true. An 18 month old cannot take care of himself. If he doesn't have someone to give him food and water, he'll die. For most of us, that someone who gave us food and water was a parent (or grandparent). So we conclude: without my parent, I will die. This parent becomes really important. He or she represents life or death. If we are abandoned by them, we die.

One time when my oldest son was about 3 years old, he was watching *Sesame Street* upstairs and it was trash day. I had to take the trash can from the back of the house around to the front. I explained to my son that I would be right back and what I was going to be doing. After a minute or so, though, totally forgetting our conversation, he noticed I was gone. He couldn't find me. So, half way around the house I heard a bloodcurdling, terrorized scream for, "MOMMY!" He was totally panicked, screaming at the top of his lungs, feeling that desperation of "I'm going to die." I rushed back inside where he was sobbing, immediately picked him up, and comforted him all the while reassuring him mommy would never leave him. We rocked in the rocker and it took at least 15 minutes for his breathing to return to normal. He had been terrified.

Now, it may be hard to believe that a 30- or 40- or 50-year-old man could feel that same kind of primal life-or-death feeling, but it's true. I've had many, many clients describe to me the utter and sheer panic they feel when their partner yells at them or threatens to leave them. They find themselves willing to do ANYTHING at the moment to stop that feeling. Whether it's flight (self-abandonment) or fight (trying to control the situation). A specific example of a fear based behavior is saying yes to something that you want to say no to, "Just to keep the peace." That is, just to keep from having to face conflict because conflict brings up lots and lots of fear.

You must learn to recognize this fear, this panic, and make a conscious choice to remember — and this sounds ridiculous — but to REMEMBER that you are an adult. You will not die. You have choice. You have power. You can take care of yourself. Our psyche transports us back in time to when we really would have died if we were left by our parent. Yet you must stop that transport and say, "Hey, wait a minute. I'm 37 years old. I will not die if she gets upset, yells, threatens, or whatever. I can take care of myself."

One of my clients who was 6'2" tall, 190 lbs., repeatedly gave up his power to his hurricaning wife (5'5", 110 lbs.). When I asked him what was going on inside, he said in disbelief, "I'm afraid she's going to HURT me." I asked, "Physically?" and he said, "Yes!" Now logically that doesn't make sense. He's bigger, stronger. He could squash her if he wanted to. Yet he cowered from her inside. Of course it turns out this man was beaten as a child if he talked back to either of his parents. So, he learned to shut his mouth and developed a fear of getting hit. Time to update his computer data. He's big now. Nobody's going to hit him, and if they did he could hit back. Defend himself.

Consult Your Rational Self

The fear doesn't go away unless you become aware of it and confront it. I've found that you must become conscious of your fear-base in order to change it. Changing it means knowing when the fear is kicking in and then consulting your rational self. I think it's always good to listen to your head (rational self) AND your heart (emotional self). When you are responding like a child, you are in fear with your untamed emotional self running wild. Bring up your rational self and begin to learn to say, "Hey, I'm okay. I'm not going to die. No matter how out of control this feels, I am still an adult. I have choices. I can leave if I want. I can walk out of this room, house, whatever. I am not trapped. I can take care of myself. I will not die." Fear is just a feeling. It will not kill you.

Again, it's time to review how to face the storm:

1. You are not a victim. Never ever. You ALWAYS have choice.

2. The realization that you have needs, too, and it's reasonable on your part to want them to be met.

3. The awareness of when your decisions are fear-based. When you are saying yes out loud and the answer is no inside, that is a fear-based decision. You must learn to recognize it, then give yourself permission to feel the fear of saying no and say no.

Tool #4 In Facing the Storm:
A Voice

The fourth tool you will need in facing the storm is a voice. You have to have a voice.

A voice means I can say what's on my mind. A voice means I can say my opinion out loud. A voice means I can disagree. A voice means I can say no when the answer is no and yes when the answer is yes. A voice means I can tell my partner what works for me — and what doesn't. I can share out loud who I am inside. I can tell my partner what my needs are. I can tell my partner when she hurts my feelings.

A voice offers some power to my life. I no longer have to hope someone reads my mind and can know what I'm thinking and feeling. This sounds absurd, I know, but this is how many men are in relationships. Silent. Now how on earth can your partner know what works for you if you don't tell her? Not talking, saying very little, limits connection. Which makes sense if your goal is to limit connection in an effort to avoid the hurricane. I want more than that for you, though. I want for you freedom, power, and the ability to love and be loved. Avoiding the hurricane is not going to get you that. Facing the storm and learning to calm the storm will. But to do this, you must learn to speak. Even when you're afraid. You must be willing to say OUT LOUD what goes on inside of you.

A Right To Privacy

That doesn't mean you don't have a right to privacy. You do. You have a right to private thoughts that you choose not to share out loud. For example, if your boss is a total jerk, it's okay to keep that thought to yourself. In fact, it's wise to. Or if your wife is looking particularly unattractive one day, it's probably kinder not to blurt that out. I'm not talking about letting go of your ability to discern what thoughts need to be edited before they come out of your mouth. Hold onto that ability — it's important. I am, however, talking about turning down your "editor." Letting some words, sentences, paragraphs get out of your head and into a voice. Otherwise, you open yourself up to a lot of misinterpretation. If you don't talk, if you don't say out loud what you are thinking (with reasonable discretion), then your partner is left to fill in the blanks. Often incorrectly.

For example, look at the figure on the next page.

What is it? We can fill in the blanks any number of ways:

My point is, a triangle is a very different picture than a school of fish. If you meant a school of fish and your wife fills in the blanks to make it an ice cream cone, you are misunderstood. You are not being heard. You are being responded to as if you had said ice cream cone — and you didn't. But you need to be honest with yourself: if you are only giving your partner three dots, you're not giving her enough information if you mean a school of fish. You're setting yourself up to be misunderstood. You're setting your partner up for frustration. You're ripening the conditions for a hurricane. So, you've got to have a voice. I love the come back to the old saying: silence is golden. It says if silence is golden, then talking is platinum. It's true. Words will help you.

More Words

Sometimes when I work with men I say, "I want you to use more words." More, that's all. More. It's amazing to me, when the environment is safe enough, how responsive they are. Eloquent. Deep. Lots of substance to what they are thinking. It amazes me and usually surprises them, too.

You are a complex person. You have a right to a voice to let that person be known. Without a voice it's as if you are doing charades trying to get people to guess what you are saying. Have you ever played that game? Have you ever felt exasperated half way through? Can't believe people can't get what you're pantomiming to them? Ever give up in the process and say forget it? That's what it's like for you and your partner in a relationship where one of you doesn't talk. Don't let that one person be you.

You've got to have a voice. And you don't need your partner's permission to have a voice. She might not like it. She might "up the ante" when you say no to something she wants you to say yes to. In fact, I would expect that to happen. I would know that she will resist your starting to speak up for yourself, stand up for yourself, share your process out loud. It will, inevitably, feel threatening to her if she's used to calling the shots while you nod your head okay. That doesn't matter. You've still got to do it. You've still got to learn to have a voice to face, and ultimately calm, the storm.

Of course, sometimes I meet men who have the gift of gab. They are very comfortable talking. If you are such a man, this section might be about learning to say the hard stuff out loud. Maybe you are able to talk and talk and talk easily, but are not able to cut to the chase. For you, I would say it's time to focus your voice. Practice saying no. Practice speaking on an emotional level. That is, practice identifying what you are feeling and say *that* out loud.

Sometimes men who speak easily take up all the room in the conversation with their words. This is not really effective in communication. If you have a voice and it's not effective, it's like having no voice at all. For you, I would say your voice has to be fine-tuned. You've got to have a voice that's effective, which, in your case, will probably mean talking less. Being more selective in your word choice.

No Voice At All

And then, of course, there are men who don't know how to have a voice at all. They have been quiet for so long — for so many, many years — that they don't even know what they think about something or how they feel about it. If you are one of these men, that's okay. You're going to have to kick-start your engine. You are going to have to realize that you don't have a voice because you've not had room to talk perhaps your whole life. In that case, be gentle with yourself. Know it will not feel natural nor come without effort on your part. You are going to have to put a lot of energy — on purpose — into speaking. I liken it to starting a train. It takes enormous amounts of energy to get the train's wheels to move half an inch. To get those wheels turning is a slow, hard process. But, as with finding your voice, soon it takes less and less energy to keep the wheels turning. They begin to propel themselves faster and faster until, before you know it, they are gliding effortlessly across the tracks at 200 m.p.h.. That's how learning to put words to your thoughts and feelings will be for you. Enormous effort will be needed at first. Don't get discouraged. With practice less and less energy will be required until speaking up will start to feel natural and even come with ease. It will happen. You are capable. You just have to start.

Start Today

Start today. Speak up one time with one sentence. That counts. Try it again tomorrow. Keep practicing it until it gets a little easier. Then try saying no to something. Something small. Just an experiment. Try it again the next day. And the next. After that, practice saying yes. But, remember, only say yes if you have checked in with yourself and the answer really is yes. If you have reservations about it or will have even the slightest resentment, then the answer is no. Practice saying it.

Buy Yourself Time

Sometimes learning to buy yourself time while you gather the courage to say no is invaluable. Practice these phrases.

- Oh, I'm not sure. Let me get back with you.

- Mmm. Really? Let me think about it.
- I can't think straight right now. I'm not sure what I think about it. I'll have to let you know.

Buy yourself time until you figure out what you do think and feel about something. It's okay to excuse yourself and go to the bathroom. Go to the bathroom, look yourself in the mirror and say, "Okay, what *does* fit for you?" Think it through, come up with an answer, figure out the words, then you can go back and talk about it with your partner.

The point is, you do not have to have an answer NOW. Just because someone asks you for an answer now doesn't mean you have to have the answer. You're allowed to think about it and figure it out. And, believe me, if you are not in the habit of having a voice, it is NORMAL to have to take some time to figure it out. It's a new skill. When we learn any new skill, we do it slowly at first. That's because we're still thinking about the steps, still registering them.

Technique

When I was 22, I was in a summer institute at the Dayton Ballet Company taking dance class. It was a program where we danced up to six days a week, six hours a day. In one particular class I remember intensely dancing a very complicated piece. When my peers and I were finished dancing, we stood around trying to catch our breaths, waiting to hear some assessment from the choreographer. She was an old, wise madam who just sat there a few minutes, silent, looking somewhat puzzled. Finally, she said, "Do it again. But this time, make it beautiful." I'll never forget those words. You see, we were stuck in "technique." What the dance steps were. Concentrating on where we were supposed to be when. Remembering, thinking, when to turn, what the next sequence of steps was, etc. And her confrontation was wonderful, "Make it beautiful." For dance is more than the steps at the right time and the right place as is any sport done at a high level. It's more than technique. It's another dimension that happens once you internalize the steps and can forget thinking about the technique. But — and this is so important to get — the technique is essential. You cannot put together a ballet — or a basketball game worth watching — without it. You have to know the steps or the plays. You have to know where to stand when. In ballet, you have to know the next sequence of steps and exit to the right when the company exits to the right, etc.

That's what it's like in learning to have a voice, learning to face the storm. You will, for a long while, be in "technique." Learning the steps, practicing and practicing the steps, *thinking* about the steps, putting in conscious effort. It will feel hard. It will feel weird. It will feel like a pain in the neck. It will feel scary, new. And it will take thinking and remembering on your part. It will take learning technique. But then — and this is the exciting part — with practice you will be able to *internalize* the process, forget about the technique (because you'll already be carrying it with you), and make it beautiful. Once you get to this point with your voice, life is good. Your relationship with your partner will have changed dramatically as will your sense of power in the world. I'm excited for you. Practice. Start today. One sentence. One paragraph. Take your time. Figure it out. *Think* about how something impacts you. Figure out the words and say them. Practice. Give yourself grace. Don't expect yourself to be good at this at first. You won't be. It'll take practice. Six months. Everyday. You can do it.

Review

Time for reviewing tools you'll need to face the storm and to look at the last tool you'll need, boundaries. The first four are:

1. *You are not a victim.* You've got to get this one. Say it over and over and over to yourself. In every situation. "I am not a victim. I have choice." Then figure out your choices and pick

the best one. If something isn't working well, remember, you are not a victim. Take action. Do it differently. Make a different choice. You are not a victim. EVER. You are capable. You are competent.

2. *You have needs and a right to expect those needs to get met.* It is normal to have physical and emotional needs. You are normal. Part of the masses. No different than me. No different than the next guy. Your blood is red. So is mine. Welcome to the human race.

3. *You must realize when your decisions, answers, words are fear-based and ask yourself what would I do if I were not operating out of fear?* Then, what keeps me from doing that? Sometimes it helps to find a mentor. Pick someone who is happily married, who has his own power, and ask yourself, how would he respond? Then say to yourself, I can do that. Then do it. Remember you will feel fear when a behavior is a new behavior. That's normal. Don't let the fear stop you. (For more help with this, you may want to read Susan Jeffers' great book, "Feel the Fear and Do It Anyway.") Recognize it, name it, figure out what you would say or do if fear wasn't stopping you, then move toward that behavior. Do it at least in a small way. Sometimes my children say to me, "But that's really *hard*." I say, "Never be afraid of hard. You can do it." Hard is nothing more than a lot of small easy steps clumped together. Figure out the small, easy task you can do to break through your fear, then do that. You can do it.

4. *You've got to have a voice.* You're allowed to have a voice. You *need* to have a voice so you won't be misunderstood. You need a voice in order to claim your personal power in this world. Without it you will always be somewhat handicapped. Pantomiming. Hoping people can guess what's important to you and what's not.

Chapter 6

Boundaries

The fifth, and last, tool you will need in order to face the storm, the hurricane, the power person in your life today and in your youth, is boundaries. This last tool is so important, it gets a whole chapter to itself. Boundaries are lines. Hold your arm out in front of you. On one side of your arm it feels good. On the other side, it feels bad. That's a boundary. A line.

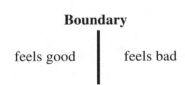

Boundary

feels good | feels bad

It's a very simple concept. Simple, not necessarily easy. But simple, nonetheless. When a person crosses over one of your boundaries, it doesn't feel good. You move from feeling good, things are fine, to hey! What just happened? Now it feels bad. When your gut stiffens, when you feel punched in the stomach emotionally, when you feel like you've been hit with a little poisonous dart (or a big spearhead), then your boundary has been crossed. Sometimes we let somebody cross over our boundary without our even knowing it. All the sudden it feels bad and we get clear one of our boundaries has been crossed. It's like with my 15 year old. We'll be rocking along and then in one moment, I'll notice he's being disrespectful in the way he's speaking to me. I usually give him grace one or two times — I mean, after all, he's 15 and he's struggling with trying to figure out life, girls, and wigging on hormones at the same time — but come the third time, I say to myself, "No, no. I don't think so. He's over the line." And I pull him back in. Pull him back to the side of the line that feels good. Pull him back to the side of speaking respectfully to me.

Consequences

And how do I do that? With consequences. For boundaries without consequences are a waste of breath. You might as well save your breath for something else. Because if you are going to have a boundary without any consequence *at all* for crossing it, then your boundary is ineffective. Period. Let's say we have a boundary in our society that stealing is illegal. In fact we do. A law that says you can't steal. Yet suppose there were NO consequence for crossing that boundary. None. Nothing would happen to you ever if you stole (not even moral-religious-wise). What do you think would happen? Need I say stealing would be rampant? Well, that Mercedes looks pretty good to me today — I think I'll take that home. No consequence, nothing. You bet, stealing would be everywhere. We might as well not even have a law that says it's illegal because it would soon become the norm. Boundaries without consequences are worthless.

So, I bring my son back over to the side of speaking with respect. How? In this case the consequence is very minor. I've stopped the behavior early on and so it's not hard to pull him back over to the other side of the line. I usually say something like, "I respect myself too much to be spoken to that way. NO ONE speaks to me that way — not my friends, not my colleagues, not my clients — and I will not have my son speak to me that way either." Then I *might* tack on something small — depending on the infraction — like "No basketball for the next hour," or, "Up to your room, please, until you can talk to me about it respectfully." Because we have always had consequences when a line is crossed, he knows the next infraction will result in a bigger consequence. It's like the police officer that issues you a warning for going 30 m.p.h. in a school zone. You drive away feeling lucky — and knowing next time you will get ticketed. Period. End of story. You are recorded in the police computer as having been stopped and given a warning. Next time you are getting a ticket. My son knows this. Chances are he'll figure out a way to talk to me about whatever it is more respectfully.

So, part of learning to have boundaries is learning how to recognize when your line is being crossed and learning how to respond to that crossing quickly and effectively.

Doormats

Boundaries (with consequences) are so important. I cannot stress this enough. They let the other person know where they stand. They create a sense of security — because the other person knows what to expect. They also create self-respect and respect from others. Think about how you feel about doormats. Do you respect them? Chances are you don't — and neither are you respected when you let your partner walk all over you.

I am working with a couple right now where the man is having difficulty "committing" and is wondering why. When I first met him I thought this could be an emotionally unavailable man. My antennae were out looking around for that possibility. But by the third session I realized a big part of the problem was the lack of boundaries on the woman's part. In the third session I asked her about something her partner had done, "Doesn't that make you feel unimportant?" to which she responded wholeheartedly, "Yes!" She then added, "but I've never felt important in this relationship." They'd been dating 18 months, mind you. I said incredulously, "Really?" and she quite matter-of-factly said, "No, never. But that's okay. I know he's busy. I know he has a life. I *understand* why I'm not that important." I was floored. This is not okay. This is a person who wants to MARRY someone she has NEVER felt important to. Whoa. I'm thinking, "Where are your boundaries, girl?" Of course this man is having trouble committing! How can you respect someone who says it's okay with me that I'm not important to you? Let alone marry her?! It's okay with me that you don't value me much. Yeah, right.

Boundaries. So important. Without them you encourage your partner to disrespect you, treat you like a doormat, hurricane. And remember, if you were not taught boundaries as a child, be gentle with yourself when realizing you don't know how to have effective boundaries as an adult. We'll go through it step by step.

The Steps

You may already know some of these steps and not others. That's fine. Take what you like and leave the rest. I know I'm starting at an elementary level. I do this because I meet many, many men who need to learn the basic, foundation level. I say this because if you are clueless about setting and enforcing effective, appropriate boundaries, you are not alone. It isn't like everyone knows how to do this and you don't. LOTS of people don't know how to do this. LOTS. I am reminded of a time when I called up one of my childhood friends, now separated by 1000 miles, who is one of my soul-sisters. We both grew up with alcoholic fathers in dysfunctional families. As children we bonded at a very deep level, understanding each other's silent suffering. On this particular day, I called her and realized how depressed she sounded. She was on her second marriage and admitted to me that he, too, like her first husband, was an alcoholic and abusive. I emphatically, desperately said to her, "Pam, you've got to go to Al-Anon. You've got to get help. *Please* promise me you'll go to Al-Anon." There was a long silence before she said, "You don't understand, Pat. I can't even get out of bed."

And then I understood at a deep level just how paralyzed she was and how absurd my request was. It was as if I were asking her to do advanced algebraic equations while she was in kindergarten trying to make sense out of counting to 100. So I threw that request out and started in kindergarten. I said to her, "Okay. Today, while I'm on the phone, Pam, will you get up and get the phone book and bring it back to bed with you?" She agreed. Then little by little over the next couple of weeks and several phone calls, we walked through step by step. Look up the Al Anon number. Get a pen and paper. Write it down. Call Al Anon and hang up. Call Al Anon and ask them the time and place of a meeting close to you. Write it down. Today get out the city map and locate it. Today drive there — don't stop, just drive by. Today drive there and sit in the parking lot 10 minutes. Etc., etc. until she was able to overcome her fears and get into action.

So we will begin the process of boundary setting. In kindergarten — working toward graduate school.

Developing Effective Boundaries

There are whole books written about boundaries. This is not one of them. So if after reading this whole section on boundaries you want further help with them, please refer to the suggested readings list at the end of this book. You've got to get this. Without boundaries you are toast. Period. It's that important.

Step One — The first step in learning boundaries is to become aware of when your boundary, your line, is being crossed. You don't have to DO anything — just become aware of it. It will feel bad. Don't skip that beat. Sometimes when our lines are crossed, and we are used to it because it happens so frequently that it feels normal to us, we barely feel the boundary violation, if at all. I want you to start tuning into your gut and become aware of the feeling that happens when your line is crossed. It won't feel good, it might feel rude, violating, invasive, hurtful, wrong.

Step Two — Begin to be aware of the jab and then — Step 2 — LA-BEL IT. When someone makes a joke at your expense, instead of just saying to yourself, "Asshole," " Bitch," say, too, "Boundary." Be aware he/she just crossed over your line, over your boundary.

You don't have to do anything else. You don't have to say anything or do anything. Just feel it, label it. Recognize that your boundary was crossed and acknowledge that to yourself. Nothing more. Simple enough? Are you willing to do it? Are you willing to practice this for a few days?

Step Three — The next step, number three, is to give yourself credit for having recognized and labeled the boundary violation. Say yeah, good job. Good for me. This counts. I'm doing good. Step 3 is learning to be on your own side. It is learning to BE WITH yourself in your process. Be present. Be your own coach. If you are not used to giving yourself compliments or hearing them from anyone else, this will seem strange, weird. It may even feel stupid. Keep practicing it. You've got to get rid of whoever's voice is beating you up — your mother's? Your father's? Perhaps a grandparent's? Replace it with your voice saying, "Good job." After you have practiced these three steps for a while — feeling it, labeling it, and giving yourself credit — it's time to start thinking of Step 4.

Step Four — Step 4 in boundary setting involves figuring out — in retrospect — what you could have said or done. What words would you have liked to have said? Would they have been helpful? Would they get you the result you want? If not, you must figure out what words WOULD have been helpful. If your wife says to you, "You're not a man. You're just like another child!" I consider that a boundary violation. It's rude, it's disrespectful, it's unloving, and unkind. Is it okay for you to be treated that way? No! So, in retrospect — not at the moment — you must figure out what words would have helped you. "F— you, bitch!" probably aren't them. There may be a part of you that wants to say that — that's normal — but when you think about it, will it get you what you want? Will it get you the love and respect that would feel so good? Will it get you a harmonious, win-win marriage? *Au contraire*. You are working on lose-lose if you respond in such a way. So what words could have HELPED you? Helped you feel good about yourself, helped you hold onto your self-dignity, and helped you change the imbalance of power in your relationship?

First of all, there's not ONE right answer. There are lots of right answers. This is the place where you brainstorm. Guess. Try things on. Remember, this is a process you are doing by yourself, in your head. Thinking. Figuring out. Remember, too, you are competent. You are capable. You can come up with a good answer. So often when I ask one of my clients, "What could you have said?" they respond with, "I don't know." GONG. WRONG ANSWER. You've got to know. This is the time in your life to know. How old are you? How old do you have to be before you know? The time is now. P.S. Nobody is born "knowing." They have to think it through and figure it out. You have a good brain. You can figure it out just like other people do. THINK. So, let's come up with some options. Brainstorm. Remember, some answers will be better than others. Some wouldn't have worked at all. That's okay. This is a time to guess.

Here are some options of words that *might* have been helpful (no guarantees — sometimes you have to try many keys to open the door).

- That's so insulting to me. Are you really wanting to insult me or are you wanting our marriage to get better?

- I'm sorry. I don't want you to have that experience. I understand what you're talking about. I've acted like a child and I'm committed to changing that.

- Wow. I'm sorry that's your experience of me. I want you to have a different experience. I want you to be able to depend on me. That's my goal.

- You know, I have had childlike behavior in the past, but that's not who I am anymore. I need you to get out of the past and update your image of me. I'm not doing those behaviors anymore. I wish that would sink in for you

- How can I make it different for you? (Then validate, validate, validate what she's saying, pick one item, and commit to change that. Then CHANGE it.)

- I want to hear what you are upset about, but I can't hear well when you are insulting me. Can you say it in a different way?

Remember, in this step you are not actually talking about it to your partner. You are not actually SAYING these words to her — you are THINKING them. You are, in your head, trying on different responses that might have been helpful and effective.

Step Five — After you've practiced this step for a bit — 2 weeks, 3 weeks — then it's time to do the next step in boundary setting, Step 5, which is learning to say the words out loud AFTER the incident. Going back and talking about it to your partner when she is in a relatively calm place. Now I don't know you. I don't know your partner. I don't know how escalated your relationship is as far as damage, so I don't know which of the above — if any — would be appropriate or helpful. But you do. Try different ones on and be aware of the results. If you feel you need help at this step, get a therapist to help you. The main thing is TRY words out. This is like a science experiment. Experiment. Note what encourages the storm. Note what calms it down.

Step Six — If any of the above escalates the situation, you MUST be willing to draw a strong line, Step 6, that says, "You must stop verbally abusing me. I will not talk to you if you are going to throw verbal insults at me. I want to talk about it — but not be called names in the process." If the insults continue, you MUST leave the room and/or house making it clear you will no longer put up with verbal abuse. You must make it clear that you are not running — you'd be glad to stay and talk about things if she will speak to you respectfully — but that you will NOT stay to be verbally abused or beaten up. The message needs to be: I want to hear you but I will NOT be verbally abused. Give her a chance or two to self-correct. If she is unable to, you MUST refuse to be verbally abused and remove yourself. Remember, you are doing a science experiment — don't let your anger get involved. So many men I work with say, "That's hard." No kidding. Of course it's hard. That's the WORK part that's needed to make an effective change in your life. Change does not magically happen just by wishing.

In fact, the kind of change I'm talking about— where you get your personal power, feel free, feel happy, and are able to give and receive love — isn't going to happen without focused effort. It's not going to come automatically, naturally. What comes automatically, naturally, is what you've already been doing. And it hasn't worked. I've heard Harville Hendrix, author of *Getting the Love You Want*, say, to respond in a conscious way — purposefully with clear thought — is somewhat counter-instinctual. It's NOT what comes automatically. What has come automatically to you — fight or flight — HASN'T WORKED.

Ping-pong

Another way of putting it is learning not to play ping-pong. Ping-pong is where couples shoot insults, snide remarks, poisonous darts, blame, back and forth, back and forth between each other. She says something rude, you say something rude back, she responds with an even deeper cut, you make fun of it, etc. Back and forth, back and forth. Have you noticed this is not effective in creating a loving, mutually respectful marriage? It IS effective in creating damage, wreckage. If that's your goal, then ping pong is the way to go. But if having your authentic power and love in your life is your goal, you must learn how to let the ping pong ball fly past you, WITHOUT hitting it back. Again, "That's hard." Yes, it's hard. It's counter-instinctual. But very important.

Step Seven — Step 7 in boundary setting is practicing *responding* to a ping-pong ball in the moment, *but not shooting the ball back.* Having an effective voice in the moment. Admittedly, this is very advanced, mature behavior. It will take practicing the first six steps a while before you are able to do Step 7. But you will get here — keep trying.

So often when I tell clients that they must learn NOT to play ping-pong, and to let the ball fly by without shooting back, they hear: be a doormat, be silent, suck it up, just take it. That's not what learning how "not to play ping-pong" means. I'm not saying, "Do not respond to a ping pong ball," I'm saying, "Do not respond to a ping-pong ball by shooting the ball back." Yes, you must respond to it —but do not play the game. When you are playing ping-pong with your partner, exchanging put downs or poisonous darts, you are getting no where as far as making your relationship better. You are getting somewhere in making it worse. If you learn to let the ball fly by you and how to respond in a purposeful way, THEN you can effect change in the system. How do you do this? Call yourself on it when you're playing. That is, be honest with yourself and admit to yourself when you're playing. Then stop. Close your mouth and walk away. In your private space figure out better words to say.

What I'm talking about is learning the difference between being *proactive* (responding) and being *reactive*. Playing ping-pong is reactive. It comes automatically. The WORK part is learning to take a breath, let the ball fly by you, figure out words that would be helpful, and SAY THEM. (You've got to have a voice.)

Proactive Thinking

In Stephen Covey's books, *Seven Habits of Highly Effective People* and *Seven Habits of Highly Effective Families*, his first habit is: be proactive. He goes on to say that if you do not develop this habit then you can forget the rest of the book. Without learning to become proactive it is impossible to change your system. It is impossible for you to get your personal power. You MUST learn how to respond (be proactive — purposeful) instead of reacting. People will say ridiculous things to you. In order not to REACT to them (blurting out a comeback without really thinking about it) there must be a beat — a pause — where you turn on your brain and THINK. Hear what the person is saying, THINK, then respond.

Proactive responding is a slower process than reacting. Proactive responses often start with validating what you've just heard. This is done by simply reflecting back, like a mirror, the exact words you just heard. "So you're saying . . ." then repeat back what you heard. For example, "So you're saying you think I'm being irresponsible?" When your partner shouts, "Yes! You are!" then you can still be thinking, "Is what she's saying true? Accurate? Is her perception off? Is that my experience? Why is it hers? AM I being irresponsible?" If you conclude you are, you can say to your partner, "You're right. That was irresponsible. I'm sorry. I need to change that." If you conclude it wasn't irresponsible, you can say that, "Gee, I can see you are really upset so I believe you that it seems irresponsible to you. But, really, I thought it through and I'm okay with my decision. I'm not sure why it's causing you pain. Can you help me understand?"

If you keep getting interrupted you can try in a polite voice, "I'm trying to change our communication style. I need you to hear my point of view. Are you willing to listen to it?" Remember, your goal is to improve things. Be clear with your partner where your boundaries are, do not play ping pong, and be responsive rather than reactive. Work on having your whole self present: your personal power, your emotions, your voice, and your boundaries.

To review, in facing the storm, take your 5 tools with you:

1. *You are not a victim.*
2. *You have needs and the right to expect those needs to get met.*
3. *Get conscious of your fear-based thoughts and actions.*
4. *Have a voice.*

5. *Have boundaries.* You won't be good at facing the storm at first. It will not go smoothly. It will be scary. That's okay. Expect it. You'll feel like you're bungling along at first. You will be. Don't get discouraged. Practice. Remember, the first time you swung a baseball bat you probably didn't hit a home run.

Chapter 7

FOO (Family of Origin)

This chapter is not about blaming your parents. It's about understanding your past. It's about seeing your past realistically. I'm not into blame. If you are, blame Adam and Eve. Because your parents got what they got from their parents who got what they got from their parents who got what they got from their parents, etc., back to the beginning of time. If you have children, you are parenting them with the skills you have. Your parents parented you with the skills they had, and their parents parented them with the skills they had, etc. Let's do a little history review of parenting.

Freud

One hundred years ago Sigmund Freud presented an outlandish, crazy concept that what happens to us as kids impacts us as adults. It was a newfangled idea. By the way, most of the other stuff Freud said I think has limited merit, but his idea that how children are treated will impact them later in life, is one that I fully embrace. Before 100 years ago, children were treated as property, and as little adults. They could be sent to work full time, beaten, and even used for sexual gratification. Incest, of course, was still culturally shunned, but nonetheless, was not thought of as *damaging* to the child.

In fact, all of this was generally believed not to be harmful to the child or to affect him in any long-term way. So here comes Freud with this controversial thought that it DOES affect the child long term. That was only four generations ago. That was the time of my great grand-parents raising my grandparents. Most people at the time didn't jump on the bandwagon and say, "Oh, Freud's right! I'd better be careful what I'm doing to my children because it will help determine who they are as adults!" No, most people hadn't even heard of Freud, and those who had, thought he was either a little off his rocker or a brilliant intellectual far removed from ordinary life. Therefore, people continued to treat their children as property and little adults.

The "Good Old Days"

My grandparents worked the fields long hours. The girls went to school through third grade then were put to work. Corporal punishment was plentiful. "Spare the rod, and spoil the child" was a common mindset. At the same time, boys were taught to be "men" and to cut off from their emotions. So, we take these two people, my grandmother and grandfather (or your grandmother and your grandfather) who married in the 1920's, and they become parents. Let's face it, their parenting skills were limited. They believed children should be seen but not heard. They believed in liberal use of corporal punishment. The father was distant, unavailable, gone a lot, working. The mother raised the children somewhat alone with little influence from her husband.

My parents were born (and yours). My father was taught to suck it up. My mother was taught to repress her sexuality. My mother was taught "sex" was a dirty word never spoken. Raised through the Depression, my parents learned survival, heartache, and shame. They learned to work hard, be thrifty, and to fight for freedom. This generation was the Battle of the Bulge generation where there were 77,000 Allied casualties in less than six weeks. Men were taught not to talk about it. Suck it up. So my parents' generation married and had children.

Not About Blame

Should I BLAME my parents for not knowing how to be avail-able? My stepfather, who raised me since I was four years old, came from a family where his biological father committed suicide when he was two. He was then raised by an alcoholic, angry stepfather who shunned him since he was not his biological child. He spent most of his time out of the house, avoiding his stepfather's drunken wrath. Should I BLAME my stepfather because he didn't know how to par-ent well? *Please.*

This is not about blame. This is about understanding. Did my step-father know how to parent well? No, absolutely not. How could he? Did it impact me in a negative way? You bet. But is it his FAULT? No way. This chapter is about looking at where your parents came from — what were THEY taught? And realizing what skills (and lack of skills) they brought with them.

Not About Denial

Now because my stepfather didn't *mean* to parent poorly, because he didn't *mean* to have poor parenting skills, because he was ill-equipped to parent well because he wasn't parented well, doesn't make it any less so. He did parent me poorly with limited skills, limited consciousness, limited awareness. Did he do it on purpose? No. Do I blame him? No. Did it happen to me? Yes. Did it impact me long term? Absolutely. Have I been able to separate and individuate from it as an adult and claim power over it? Yes. But it took a long time. The wounds were deep. And it took looking realistically at the parenting I got and OWNING that before I could break away from it. You must do the same.

Let me repeat, when looking at your family of origin, we are not looking to place blame. We are looking for understanding. You do not have to get angry at your parents. Though you might. You do not have to discuss your process with them. Though you might. You do not have to get THEM to get it. You do have to get real about it: You weren't raised at Ozzie and Harriett's. None of us were. Look at the history of parenting these past 100 years.

A Closer Look At No Wounds

Sometimes I have a client who says, "I had a great childhood. No wounds. My parents were great. They loved me. Really, I had a perfect childhood." Now if that were true, that'd be great. But why, then, is this man in therapy disconnected from his emotional self, unable to commit to marriage, or feeling "trapped"? Why then am I hearing "victim?" Reactionary? Or why is his wife in so much pain? Why does he have two divorces in his history? Why is his brother unable to hold down a job — or has a drug problem? One of my clients who told me how normal and wonderful his childhood was, had a brother in jail for robbing banks! Plural — BANKS! I'm sorry, this does not come out of a highly functional childhood.

Admittedly, when I began my own recovery process at age 19, I thought my family was the Ozzie and Harriett Nelson family. After all, my mom told us that. I thought we were this great, high functioning, no problems family. Denial is strong. It took me some time to get that my father was an alcoholic, my stepfather was there but not there, my mom was controlling (a common coping mechanism for an out of control situation), that I had been sexually abused since I was very young, that my father had affairs, that my mom was on Valium . . . need I go on? I could see none of this. I believed we were the happily ever after family and that there was something wrong with ME because I couldn't seem to get it together. I defended my parents vehemently. Especially my father who was the most abusive to me. It took me years before I could see him realistically: as the sociopathic, alcoholic, power person he was my entire childhood.

How About You?

What happened to you? Who were your parents and where did they come from? What kind of parenting did they get growing up? I'm going to assume that your parents did the very best they could with the information they had. I'm going to assume that they did the very best they could with the parenting skills and the level of consciousness they had. I'm going to assume they loved you (because most parents really do love their children) and that their hearts were in the right place. I'm going to assume they were good people — most people are. But I'm not going to assume, because all of that was true, that they were good parents. Good people, yes. Good parents, not necessarily. People can only parent with the skills they have and if they weren't parented well, they did not have good skills to parent you well. Period. That has NOTHING to do with whether or not they were good people. Remember, we are looking at the parenting you got — not sitting in judgment trying to place blame.

So, did you have a raging parent? An absent one? An emotionally unavailable one? How about a power parent? Or one that just didn't have good parenting skills though they tried really hard? How about an emotionally incestuous one? Let's look at emotional incest for a moment because it is HUGE. It is something I see so frequently that it probably helps define our society at this point.

Emotional Incest

If you were the chosen child, the favorite, the hero child in your family, this section is very important. It may have felt like your childhood was ideal. After all, who can complain about being adored by their parents, given special privileges, being the one looked up to for the answers, being the smart one, being the responsible one? It can be a pretty comfortable and flattering place to be. Especially if you had a sibling that was "difficult." These are the clients who say my childhood was great, my parents both loved me, I didn't really have any "wounding." And again, that would be believable if the rest of the pieces of their lives reflected that. Especially their significant relationships. That is not my experience. I have found that the "chosen child" is often the most damaged, most wounded, most disconnected from his feelings, most frightened of connection.

Pat Love coined the term "emotional incest" in her book, *The Emotional Incest Syndrome*. If you were the "chosen child" in your family, I highly recommend your reading it. In my experience, after studying her book, after watching this phenomenon in my office daily for years, I have come to define emotional incest as, "when the parenting energy is backwards." That is, in a healthy environment, it is my job to take care of the emotional needs of my child. In an emotional incestuous environment, it is my child's job to take care of MY needs. In other words, it's the child's job to make me happy, make me proud, listen to my problems, be my confidant, do what I like to do, excel in my interests, be my best friend, my buddy. In emotional incest, the parent doesn't *parent* the child, he/she *befriends* him. If you were the chosen child, the hero, the favorite, you may have emotional incest to look for in your history.

Remember, this is not about blame. It's about understanding. These are clues I look for in determining if a man has been emotionally incested in childhood:

1. First, he claims an ideal childhood — and yet his marriage/ relationship is not working in a severe way.

2. He has an underground "secret life" — more often than not this involves acting out sexually but always involves hiding things and lying (especially through omission).

3. He has a "split" in his view of himself — it is overinflated and includes a sense of entitlement (I'm special so the world owes me or I'm special so that rule doesn't apply to me) AND it is under-inflated and includes a sense of worthlessness (no matter what I do it's never good enough).

4. A common response to conflict is staring and saying nothing:

he has the "deer caught in the headlights" response, OR, he vehemently defends his position.

5. I also look for family situations that were "ripe" for emotional incest. For example, a single parent raising a single child can often — but not necessarily — lead to emotional incest. A "dead" marriage where the wife is not getting her emotional needs met by her husband often leads to emotional incest. So often the wife turns to a son in this scenario to get her needs met. This is very common. Why? Because husbands have historically been taught to *cut off from their feelings*, and remember, if a person is not connected to his feelings, he cannot meet the emotional needs of his partner. So, the husband's not there for the wife, and thus she turns to this adorable child into which she can pour all her emotions, hopes, and dreams. And when the little boy grows up, is it any wonder he feels "suffocated" and/or "trapped" when a woman wants to emotionally connect with him? Unfortunately, this perpetuates the cycle. For now we have the next generation man who is unable to be emotionally available to *his* wife who in turn turns to *her* child, etc., and the cycle goes on.

The Best Intentions

This is usually NOT a conscious process. People do not on purpose say: I think I'll "love" my child too much and screw him up. No one would do that. Emotional incest happens usually very innocently. The parent doesn't realize he or she is hurting the child. I believe most parents, if they were made aware of how they were damaging their child through emotional incest, wouldn't do it! They'd stop. In other words, I'm saying emotional incest comes from ignorance — not knowing, not understanding — and not from maliciousness.

But it's damaging nonetheless.

The more severe the emotional incest, the more hidden it is from the recipient. In other words, if the emotional incest was thorough, began at birth, then it just seems "normal." It's all the child ever knew. If the emotional incest started at age 14 when his parents divorced, then it's more easily recognized and worked on. The more damaged of my clients are the ones where the emotional incest was always there. Two cases come to mind, though I could easily list 100.

Case #1

The first was a second-generation Holocaust survivor. Both his parents had been in Nazi concentration camps. His mother lost her first husband and two children there. His father lost his entire family of origin, all but one sibling. So after the war these two meet and marry. Soon she gets pregnant — and can you imagine the expectations put on this child? To make everything okay, to make life worth living again, to make them happy and take away the pain. And too, since they were older, they knew this would be their only child. Emotional incest started at conception for this man! He didn't stand a chance.

Case #2

This man's father shipped off to fight a war in Korea leaving behind a very pregnant wife. Two years later he returns home to find he has a two year old son, a stranger for a child, who clings to mommy. Not to mention the two-year-old stage in a child's life is often not the most attractive one. His wife becomes pregnant again and has son #2. Guess which one's "Daddy's boy"? Son #2 gets latched onto from the second dad gets that first smile from him. THIS is his son. The older boy, now three, continues to be shunned by the father while son #2 gets doted on. Eventually son #1 incurs his father's rage and wrath while son #2 remains adored. The cycle has begun.

Both of these men would grow up feeling "special" and that the "rules" of life didn't really pertain to them. Both men remained very childlike in their thinking — that good things should just magically happen to them. That they should start at the top; that they should be allowed to skip steps. Both men were in marriages where they gave their power away to their partners and then went underground. Both men ran up great debt, both men cheated on their wives, both men rationalized and minimized these behaviors. This is the damage emotional incest can do. There's an arrogance with it. A cockiness, a self-righteousness. And there's a victim attitude at the same time. "I'm trapped," "My wife won't let me," "I didn't get the promotion because they are assholes," and lots of silence. Underground.

No real power. Pseudo power. If this sounds like you, or your wife or partner is saying, "This is you! This is you!" — pay attention. Let's take a moment to look at Johari's Window.

Johari's Window

Johari's Window was named after two researchers, Joseph Luft and Harry Ingram. In 1955 they designed an educational model for group process. This model describes our self-knowledge as divisible into four quadrants, like a windowpane. These quadrants are Open, Hidden, Blind, and Unknown. The Open quadrant shows all the parts of ourselves that are known to self and known to others. The Hidden quadrant shows the parts of ourselves that are known to self but unknown to others. The Blind quadrant holds all those things that are known by others but unknown to ourselves. And finally, the Unknown quadrant is filled with everything that is unknown to self and unknown to others. Following is a picture with an example of information that might be contained in each quadrant.

An example of a repressed memory may be that a person is unable to recall what happened in between his car skidding off the road and being aware he was in the hospital.

Open	Hidden
(Known to Self, Known to Others)	(Known to Self, Unknown to Others)
I am married.	I am terrified of snakes.
Blind	**Unknown**
(Unknown to Self, Known to Others)	(Unknown to Self, Unknown to Others)
I am an alcoholic.	Repressed Memories

The Blind Quadrant

When I ask, "Did you have emotional incest in your history? Were you the chosen child?" and you say, "I don't think so," but your wife says, "YES!" this is an example of the Blind quadrant. Pay attention if your wife says, "This is you!" People can see things about you that you cannot see about yourself. This may be the key you need to unlock your armor.

And I mean ARMOR. Thick, solid, steel armor. The emotionally incested child, feeling invaded at some level, violated somehow, begins to put on armor to protect himself. He learns how to be the apple of his parent's eye by squirreling away little pieces of himself. He learns not to show certain sides of himself lest he be replaced in the "special" role. Later it's easy to slip into not telling the whole story — removing any parts that would make him look bad. This is usually not a conscious process. If it starts young enough, I venture to say it is never a conscious process. Subconsciously, the child keeps pieces of himself to himself. When a parent "loves" the child too much, he builds walls to keep the "real him" safe. I had a client who, at 38, drew me this picture of his childhood:

When I asked for an explanation he said, pointing to the dot, "This was me," and to the large circle, "And this was my mother." A sadness washed over me. Then he added, "And I was never allowed outside of the circle." Small wonder he felt "trapped" whenever a woman got too close to him.

The Pebble

Another one of my clients never understood an odd habit he had as a child. He remembers daily trying to wake up very early in the morning — before his mother — and sneaking out of the house each day to find a pebble. He would then hide the pebble as best he could. "Then at the end of the day I would check the hiding place, and if it was still there, I knew that my mother hadn't gotten that piece of me. Somehow I felt comfort in that." This man was the favorite son of a woman who was in a lonely, dead marriage. She turned to her son — unwittingly — to get her emotional needs met. And he, bless his heart, tried to cope. Tried to protect himself from being devoured. When I met this man he was married — and spent most of his time doing destructive things to the marriage hoping his wife would throw him out. Here lies the complexity of emotional incest.

Emotional Impotence

When a little boy is emotionally incested — particularly by his mother — he doesn't develop a sense of power — especially in regard to women. Here is a man feeling trapped in his marriage, "controlled" by his wife, acting out destructively against the marriage (lying mostly), who feels impotent to change the situation. He doesn't believe he even has the power to leave the marriage — he must wait until his wife throws him out. He doesn't know he has any power in the marriage to CHANGE IT. To change it by ending it or change it by healing it. He feels like that little boy, of course, never allowed outside of the circle. Having experienced years of not being able to influence the system with his mother, he believes (emotionally) that the situation is the same with his wife. He continues to ACT as he did as a child — even though he is now an adult and has choices.

This feeling of impotence so often leads to acting out sexually: going to topless clubs, going to porn shops, doing porn on the internet, going to massage parlors. It's a primitive way to overcome this feeling of emotional impotence. After all, a man can go to a topless club and pick from a number of women (feels powerful) to have them strip for him (feels powerful). Yet, of course, it's only pseudo power because without dropping the bucks, his "potency" is nonexistent.

I once worked with a man who spent $3,000 *per week* at one particular topless club. That's a lot of money. In fact, he spent all of his income there. He was married with three children and professed to love his wife and want a good marriage. Of course his sexually addictive behavior was doing everything BUT creating a good marriage. It was destroying it. I decided to take two tactics. First, to have his wife come in with him; and second, to challenge him not to spend one dime at the club for seven days. He agreed to do both.

Two days later he brought his wife in for a session. She was very cold and VERY angry. Not surprisingly. She proceeded to tell me what a complete and utter F-up her husband was and began a long litany of his lying and cheating and being a lousy husband and a lousy father, etc. If I had let her, she would have swirled into a full-blown hurricane (which she did at home on a regular basis). She made all the decisions in the house — because she couldn't count on him. She paid all the bills with her meager income. She confessed she raged at him daily because he wasted all his money and left her to be the only financially responsible adult in the house. The husband, in the meantime, tried to speak up a couple of times only to be quickly silenced by her wrath. He sat on the couch like a little boy letting her give him the "whipping" he deserved. The session confirmed my suspicions. Here was a man who felt no personal power in his relationship. He felt completely unable to make any impact on the situation. Emasculated. Impotent. Childlike. Much like how he felt as a child with his mother who smothered him. It wasn't surprising that he chose topless bars as his venue where he could feel "powerful" with women.

He also is a good example of the "split" that happens so often with men. That is, some men are able to be very effective in the work world – this man earned over $150,000 per year – and yet completely childlike in their interpersonal relationship world. Again, here is the complexity of the damage from emotional incest.

The second part of his experiment, not spending one dime in the club for a week, brought this man to a higher level of self-honesty. The "girls" started paying less and less attention to him as the week wore on and went on to other "prospects." The manager showed concern for my client's sales, "How's your business doing?" but not for my client. His "world" began to crumble and come into clearer focus. He decided to try the experiment a second week though this was harder than the first week because he was so craving a "fix" where he could feel "powerful" again. He did it though, and by the end of the second week, the girls were "friendly" to him but left him to sit alone at his table while they looked for better game. Thus began his recovery process. Thus began his quest for authentic personal power and recovery from his childhood emotional incest.

It Was Not Your Fault

So, what happened to you? Was there emotional incest in your family of origin? Please know if there was, it was not your fault. Envision a sweet little boy sitting quietly in the back seat of the car looking at his comic books while his parents are in the front seat arguing. It doesn't matter who's driving, mom or dad. Maybe one of them has been drinking, maybe not. But they're arguing. Distracted. Suddenly a car pulls out in front of them, they swerve, but too late. And you, the little boy in the back seat, get crushed. You have two broken legs, three broken ribs, and a broken pelvis. They walk away relatively unscathed. Now, is that fair? No. Is it your fault? No. Is it your problem? Yes. That's how emotional incest is. The child really is the victim. If you have this in your history it is not your fault even remotely, but it is your problem. You're going to have to wear the casts, sit in the wheelchair, do the physical therapy, and learn to walk all over again. You're going to have to face your emotional incest and do battle with it if you don't want it to rule your life.

Battling Emotional Incest

If you were emotionally incested as a child, intimate relationships will be hard for you. In facing this, there are three responses to consider. To understand them, it may be helpful to, believe it or not, put yourself into the shoes of an Olympic cross country skier.

Let's say you have made the Olympic Cross Country Ski Team and the day has arrived to get on the plane and go to the games. You are so excited! This is a dream come true. You arrive at the sight of the Winter Games and excitement is oozing out of your every pore. There are thousands of people there. You are meeting the best of the best athletes of the whole world. What a privilege, what an honor. You are in awe of everything. And then come the opening ceremonies where you walk in the parade with your country. It is an amazing experience. It's so beautiful. It's magnificent. It all feels a little surreal. You have to pinch yourself to make sure it's really happening.

And then it's time to wait. Wait for the day of your race. Mentally prepare. Concentrate. Get focused. Study the course. Calm down and get ready to work. Finally the day arrives. All the skiers, including yourself, take off with gusto. Each wants to win that gold medal. And now the work begins. You must ski hard. You must ski smart. Save your energy for the up hills. Concentrate. Push yourself. Set yourself up for a pass. Pass the next person. Pass the next person. You're exhausted, but keep pushing, plotting, passing. You doubt yourself and then push that doubt away. Work harder you say to yourself. Finally, you're safely ahead of the pack. You have one more skier to overtake. Just one.

Here's where all that you've worked toward for years finally comes completely together. Your body is working like a fine tuned machine. You can taste the victory. You know you've got it. You're practically flying at this point. Everything is working beautifully. You can see the finish line. It's time to pass the last skier and you go for it. There is no doubt in your mind any longer. YOU will win the gold. And you do!

As the skier you've gone through three distinct phases. Phase I: The Arrival. It's great. It's exhilarating. The excitement of it all, the fun, the majesty. Phase II: The Race. This is the hard part. You work, and you work, and you work. Phase III: The victory. You let your body take over and do what you know you can do. It's sweet. It's wonderful. You are so grateful. You hold the gold.

Stuck In Phase I

Now, back to emotional incest. One response people have to emotional incest is to spend their lives going from relationship to relationship to relationship, ever stuck in Phase I. Here the relationships are new and exciting. They are fun, wild and crazy even. Talking is easy, sex is easy, adrenalin pumps into your every fiber. It is the "falling in love" stage of a relationship. It is great — until your partner starts to have needs. And wants.

As soon as she wants safety or commitment, the emotionally

incested man begins to feel uncomfortable, even trapped. He pushes away, maybe even runs away. He has to get out, feeling that if he doesn't, he'll surely suffocate. He breaks up (or does so many destructive things that she breaks up with him) and goes on to the next girl. Whew. A new beginning. A breath of fresh air. He can never get to Phase II where the relationship develops its depth through hard work. And, sadly, he can never taste the sweet victory of Phase III where he and his partner are in sync so beautifully.

Pseudo-Marriage

A second response to emotional incest is, after many beginning relationships and lots of razzing from friends and relatives, the man decides to get married. It's time. All his friends are. He's the last hold out. He has fun with the girl he's dating, so, why not? And he gets married. Only not really. As soon as he says "I do," that feeling of trapped or being controlled or suffocation begins to swell. He runs for his life *in the marriage.* That is, having no sense of authentic power, he may go underground. Have an affair, start going to clubs, lying, flirting with other women, going to topless bars, gambling with his buddies, not coming home after work with no explanation. He starts doing everything he can to "get space." The wife ends up feeling punished and treated like an intrusive, controlling big, bad witch when all she wants is a partner. Her reasonable expectations of partnership seem outrageous to the emotionally incested man who goes the marriage route without first having addressed his emotional incest.

Sandy and Tom

Sandy described her first year of marriage to Tom. Before they were married, Tom adored her, couldn't get enough of her. Called, romanced, and coddled her. She loved it, of course. Then, shortly after they got married, Tom seemed to "go away." This was Tom's third marriage, not surprisingly. He had two children who came to stay with them for the summer. During their stay, Tom wanted to have regular family dinners with the kids. Sandy asked him when would be a good time for him to come home from work and eat dinner. He said six o'clock.

So, Sandy set about each day to have a nice, homemade dinner ready for Tom and his two kids and her at six o'clock. Then emotional incest repercussions set in. Tom became furious. He said Sandy was trying to control him by making him eat at the same time each night. To counter this, even if he was home at six o'clock, he would not eat with the family. He decided to take his food into the family room and watch TV because he wasn't going to be told how and when to eat. Sandy, in the meantime, said she wasn't trying to control him at all, and that they didn't have to stick to the six o'clock time. She was willing to have dinner ready at any time. She was willing to be flexible and have dinner ready at different times on different days. She was willing for Tom to completely call the shots on the time. Still Tom fumed. He began coming home at ten o'clock some nights, not calling but just not showing up for dinner. Sandy was stunned. She decided the children needed more consistency and began, once again, to serve dinner at six o'clock for herself and Tom's two children. Tom, because of the emotional incest in his history, began to feel Sandy was trying to steal his children from him. And Sandy was just trying to serve healthy family meals as TOM had requested! Thus is the power of emotional incest.

Fight For Your Life

The third response a person can have from a history of emotional incest is to battle it. Go head to head with it. Be aware of it and learn what it looks like. Become alert when it starts to rear its ugly head and consciously decide not to run away or push away, but to stay. The movie, *A Beautiful Mind*, is based on the life of Nobel prize winner John Nash. It tells of his fight with schizophrenia: he sees and hears people who do not really exist. In a small way, that's how emotional incest is. The man who was emotionally incested as a child sees and hears threats where threats do not really exist. John Nash, in his own recovery, learned not to "give into" these voices. He learned not to believe them. He stopped giving them energy, time, attention, value, and, remarkably, completely recovered from schizophrenia.

You, like John Nash, can stop interacting with the imaginary threats you encounter in a relationship. This most readily happens through self-definition. I cannot recommend therapy highly enough for you if you have emotional incest in your history. You must work with someone who does family of origin work who is familiar with emotional incest. You must get some accurate reflecting since you were raised in a house of funny mirrors. Also, I cannot recommend the New Warrior training weekend highly enough for you, either (Suggestion #8 in the next chapter). It is a must. Another concrete behavior you can do to battle your legacy is to go to Adult Children of Alcoholics twelve-step meetings.

How I wish for you to stop running. This will happen through self-definition and the awareness that your partner wants to love you and not swallow you up. You will not disappear if you fight your emotional incest. In fact, for the first time in your life, there will be space for you.

Other Dysfunctions?

One way to help you get clear about your family of origin history is to talk to your siblings, talk to your aunts and uncles, perhaps even talk to your parents. Any of these people may have important information for you. If you are the trailblazer in your family — the first one to start questioning what didn't work in the parenting you received — you may come up against closed doors when you talk to your relatives. However, it is my experience as a therapist that almost always it is helpful to seek information from other family members. You might ask, "What do you remember about our childhood?" or "Can you tell me what you know about my father's childhood?" You may be surprised and even shocked at what you find out. Be curious. Be open. Want to know and information will come to you.

My 60-year-old aunt had a therapy session with her mother, my grandmother. The *opening words* out of my grandmother's mouth were, "Well, you know her father committed suicide." My aunt was floored. She had NEVER been told this information. It was a "family secret." She had been told for 60 *years* that her father died in a work accident. This was a critical piece of the puzzle for my aunt. Other clients report:

- I was stunned when my uncle said to me, "I hated to see how you were so grossly favored over your brother. It was really sickening."

- My sister says she won't even go to our parents' funerals.

- My brother remembers a lot of discord in the house, lots of arguing. I don't remember that at all, but my sister says the same thing.

- My aunt says my parents both drank heavily until I was 5 and then got involved in the church and just quit. She even remembers my dad hitting my mom when he was drunk.

- My grandmother says she's glad my grandfather's dead because he was a mean SOB, etc.

Honestly, you may get amazing information. And you may not. If you're the trailblazer, you might not get a lot. You'll probably get reports of how wonderful your parents were. And they probably WERE wonderful — but if you're reading this book, they probably didn't have great parenting skills. Look at their histories. Ask your parents to tell you what it was like in *their* family of origin. Again, my experience is that, more likely than not, you will get valuable information that helps you more realistically look at your own history and begin to make sense of your current behaviors.

Don't be afraid to seek out a therapist to help you, either. This is especially necessary if you keep coming up with, "Nothing. I had a great childhood," and your partner gave you this book to read. Your partner is trying to tell you something very important. Take note. And find a therapist to help you. It's like putting together a puzzle: if you have two people looking for pieces and figuring out how they go together, it goes faster than if you are building it yourself. Therapists are trained to help you figure out where your current behaviors came from and to help you change those behaviors if they're not effective.

However, a Word About Finding a Therapist

If you decide to work with a therapist — because you are at an impasse or you find the process confusing or just because you want to speed things up — be careful. Unfortunately, there are a lot of really bad therapists out there. Really bad. So you have to be selective. Do not give your power away. Be selective. Trust your gut.

1. Ask around if you can. Try to get a personal recommendation.

2. Interview them on the phone. Get a feel for them. If they aren't willing or able to give you five minutes of their time, that's a red flag for me.

3. Go in for a session. You are not committing to anything but ONE session. One hour of your time. See how you feel with him or her. See if you feel like you got anything out of the hour. If you felt relatively safe and comfortable and took away food for thought from the session, then think about going back to that person for five or six sessions. Reevaluate. You should be feeling some progress. If when you visit with someone, you do not like that person, DO NOT GO BACK. Call someone else. I know so many people who have gone to therapists *they didn't like* and I wonder Why? Go to a therapist that you like and feel has snap. Life is short. Don't waste it on a therapist who's not really helpful. Find one that is. Just know that you may have to try out a few before you find a good match. That's NORMAL.

Chapter 8

Reconnecting with Feelings

This is the most difficult chapter to write and yet is perhaps the most important one. It is the most difficult because each of you reading this book is a unique individual and thus what may work for one person won't necessarily work for another. Therefore, this chapter is going to be full of suggestions: some of which may be helpful in helping you reconnect with your feelings; others may not be helpful at all. Try one, and then try another, and so on until you get to your TEARS. Yes, tears. Chances are you are already connected to your anger— men have historically been given permission in our culture to have their anger — and that's good (as long as it's not rage). It's good, but not enough. This chapter is about getting connected to your sorrow, your grief, your hurt. I believe that those that grieve well, live well, love well. Therefore it is essential that you connect to your losses at an emotional level. Remember, the goal is to get to your tears.

This may not happen by doing one of these exercises. You may have to do ten. And if that doesn't get you there, try twenty. The point is, don't stop until you get to your tears.

The Chinese Bamboo Tree

These exercises will probably have a cumulative effect. That is, they will work like a Chinese bamboo tree. The Chinese bamboo tree is planted into fertile ground where it can get lots of sunshine. The gardener waters it and fertilizes it for a whole year. And in the first year, nothing happens. The tending continues and in the second year, nothing happens. Still the gardener waters where he planted, fertilizes, pulls the weeds. For four years, nothing happens. And then, toward the beginning of the fifth year — it grows 90 feet tall in six weeks! *World Book Encyclopedia* even cites examples of this amazing tree growing 36 inches in a 24-hour period.

I say all this because often that's how recovery of your feelings works. You have to stick with the process even when it seems like nothing is happening. When you do the exercises in this chapter, they may seem to have no impact on you. But, I tell you, keep tending the seed. Your growth will happen — but it might not show for a while. Keep working it, though. Don't give up. You are valuable and deserve to be happy. You are valuable and deserve to be loved. You are valuable and deserve to have your whole self available to you. You are sacred. You've had wounding that has created your needing to protect yourself. That's all. Now it's time to heal the wounding. Don't wait any longer. Life is passing you by. Your children need you NOW. Life is short: don't wait.

What Went Wrong?

In this chapter I want you to look at what went wrong in your childhood. Not what went right. THAT didn't wound you. What went wrong? What didn't work? Where were the gaps in your parents' parenting? What were you missing? What were your losses?

In this chapter I'm asking you to get ACTIVE. Do something. Take action. It's what therapists call "experiential" work. Where you don't just sit and talk about it, but that you actually do something. Some of these suggestions involve writing: writing thoughts out, making lists, writing letters. Writing things down on a piece of paper seems to give some people incredible clarity. You might be one of those people. Try it and see. If you are not one of those people who gets clarity from writing, don't worry about it. In general, I would say if you don't like writing exercises, don't write. Just do the exercises in your head. For me, I hate writing exercises in books. I don't, in general, ever do them. Sometimes I'll do one if it's just writing down a list. I do, however, do them in my head. This is the most effective for me. Experiment and find out what is the most effective for you.

One last thing. This may seem odd to say, but you may even get rid of constipation. Many people who are "blocked" emotionally, are "blocked" physically as well. They suffer with chronic constipation. You may be one of these people. The good news is, when you get reconnected to your feelings, when you get "unblocked" emotionally, the constipation will go away. It's a nice, often unexpected, extra perk for many people.

Again, don't stop trying different suggestions until you get to your tears.

Suggestion 1:
Adjust Your Attitude

Here you've got to get clear on the goal (to reconnect to your emotional self) and make a conscious decision to make it YOUR goal. Not my goal for you. Not your wife's goal for you. YOUR goal. Because if it's not YOUR goal, you're not going to get there. It's that simple. You can't do this work with an attitude of doing it to make your wife happy and get her off your back. The work will only be effective if *you* want to get there. There's an old story about Socrates. He is sitting on the beach meditating when a young lad approaches him and says, "Teach me, I want to learn." Socrates glances toward him and then returns to his meditation. The boy says, "Teach me. I want to learn!" Socrates looks him over and then returns to his meditating. At this point the boy practically screams in frustration, "Why won't you teach me? I want to learn!" Socrates rises and suddenly picks the boy up. He walks into the water with him. Deeper and deeper. Finally, Socrates pushes his head under the water. The boy kicks and thrashes and tries to free himself. Finally Socrates releases him. The boy gasps frantically for air and soon asks, "Why did you do that?" To which Socrates replies, "When you want to learn as much as you wanted air, then I will teach you."

Want it like air. Decide consciously, deliberately, okay, I'm going to do this work. Get honest with yourself. Don't do it halfheartedly. Don't do it half-assed. If you do, you're wasting your time. Do it sincerely because YOU believe you need to grow. Because you believe some of the things you've read in this book have rung true for you. Because you want to be a better partner, better husband, better person. Because what you have done so far hasn't worked.

I had a client one time whose wife said, "If you don't go to therapy, I'll divorce you." So he went — to me. He was an interesting man whose woundedness and pathology was blatantly apparent the very first hour we met. It was clear to me that he had major emotional work to do and that he had been severely emotionally traumatized as a child. We agreed to see each other once a week for 3–4 weeks and then for him to reevaluate whether or not he wanted to continue. He thanked me profusely for the session and made an appointment for the next week. Unfortunately, the next week something pressing came up at work, and he had to cancel at the last moment, but he rescheduled for the next week. Since I have a 24-hour cancellation policy — my clients are charged for their reserved hour if they cancel less than 24 hours in advance — he said he'd drop off a check. Which he did. The next week he had car problems and again had to cancel at the last minute, but he assured me he would drop off a check. He rescheduled.

I began to smell a rat, of course. It occurred to me that he was using his cancelled checks to "prove" to his wife that he was indeed going to therapy and that he would play this game as long as I would let him. When he rescheduled and cancelled again, I called him on his game, which he flatly denied. I said I wouldn't be able to accept any more of his checks unless he came in for a session. He was insistent and sent me a check in the mail anyway. I returned it with a polite note reiterating my position. I never heard from him again. But I did hear he had gotten another therapist — and another — and another. And lots of cancelled checks. The problem was, he never did any work. He pretended to, but he never did. His wife divorced him. You can't "fake" recovery for any length of time. It shows. When you are actually doing the work, you transform. You leave the place of fear and child ego and get your authentic adult power. Therefore, do the work and do it for you. Make it your goal.

In consciously deciding to do what it takes to reconnect to your feelings, be aware that you will be outside of your comfort zone. Decide that's okay. Your current comfort zone doesn't include being comfortable with feelings. So, any of these exercises/suggestions may very well be outside of your comfort zone. In fact, let's hope so. You want to EXPAND your comfort zone, which, of course, can only be done by going outside of what is comfortable for you right now. Make a conscious choice to go outside of your comfort zone. That is, feel the fear but do it anyway. Can you say to yourself: I know this will be uncomfortable for me at first, but I still want to do it?

Suggestion 2:
Inventory Your Losses

Do this in a very quiet, private place. Do this where you won't be interrupted. Do this alone. It should take about an hour of your time at the most. Write down all the losses you had in your childhood. These could be big or these could be small. Deaths: Relatives who died. Friends who died. Friends of the family. Pets. Dreams. Write down family moves. How often? How old were you? Losses. Losses. All kinds of losses. Didn't make the 7th grade basketball team. Your dad never came to your baseball games. You didn't ever have a girlfriend. You didn't really feel safe (loss of security). Flood. Fire. Tornado. Other natural disasters. Did your parents divorce? Who moved out? How old were you? You couldn't go to camp because your family couldn't afford it. You were sent away to boarding school. Car accidents. Really brainstorm. Some losses are very obvious (i.e., my father died when I was 12; I didn't get to go to my grandmother's funeral). Some losses are quite obscure (i.e., loss of connection with my parents because they were more interested in watching TV than talking to me; loss of serenity because my parents were always fighting; loss of safety because my older brothers always bullied me). Brainstorm. Brainstorm. Brainstorm. If you only have two on your list, keep working on it. Get more honest with yourself.

Next, take a look at each loss and write down how old you were when it happened. Then, take a look at each loss and think about how you dealt with it. Who told you about the loss? Did you cry? Were you sad? Did someone help you? Who? What were the messages you were given about it? If the loss brings up sadness for you now, let yourself feel it. Wallow in it. Deepen it. Close your eyes. Let yourself relive the loss. Connect with the pain.

Suggestion 3:
   I Deserve List

This works better if you actually write down a list rather than just think about it. This is because after you've written your list, I want you to read it to yourself at least once a day until you've memorized it and fully integrated it into your psyche. In psychological terms, assimilated it. Absorbed it. Made it part of your "Truth."

So what is an "I deserve list?" It's something like an affirmations list. It's to affirm your worth and dignity as a human being. It's a personal Bill of Rights: the right to life, liberty, and the pursuit of happiness. You will need to have at least 15-30 items on your list. Here are some ideas to get you started. However, do not put *my* ideas on *your* list unless you want to claim them for yourself. Note: You'll need to play around with the opening phrase: try "I deserve"; try "I am allowed to"; try "I have a right to." Use what works for you. It may vary from sentence to sentence. That's fine. Do what works.

- I deserve to be happy.
- I deserve to be treated with respect.

- I am allowed to say no.
- I have a right to say no.
- I deserve to be loved.
- I deserve to be touched lovingly.
- I deserve good treatment.
- I am allowed to never speak to my father/mother again.
- I deserve friendships.
- I deserve the truth.
- I deserve fidelity.
- I'm allowed to have fun.
- I deserve kind words.
- I am allowed to have financial freedom.

Fifteen items, at least. Read your list a minimum of once a day until it's memorized, integrated.

Suggestion 4:
Genogram

This is a visual chart and is most powerful when written down. You will need a big piece of paper and 10-12 different colored markers. Genograms are like a family tree. They can be really complex or relatively simple. We're going for the relatively simple here. Begin with drawing a simple family tree. Start with your grandparents (you can do great grandparents and/or great aunts and uncles if you are really ambitious).

Mark down who married who. Mark down the names of their kids, your cousins, their kids, etc. Drawing the tree is the chore part. It'll take you awhile. For most people it's not fun. Do the best you can and it will be good enough.

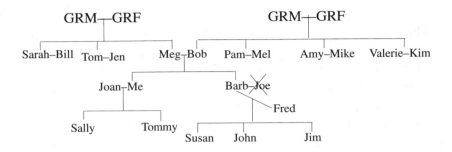

After the tree is done, I want you to make a "key" with your different colored markers. Use a different color for each of the following:

- divorces
- heavy alcohol drinking
- drug use (prescription as well as illegal)
- suicides
- affairs
- sexual abuse
- family secrets
- jail time
- heavy gambling

You can make extra categories if they apply: physical abuse, teenage pregnancy, adoptions, prostitution, bankruptcies, other types of addictions (including religion), etc. Now go back and mark on your tree each of these categories. That is, if your divorce category is red, use your red marker to indicate where divorces happened in your family tree. This is the fun part most people enjoy. It doesn't matter how you indicate each of the categories — use check marks, circles, x's, or whatever — just make sure you keep the color of each category consistent. Go through all nine categories and any extras you may have added. Be as brutally honest as you can be. Your family tree will probably look a bit chaotic or maybe even extremely chaotic. That's okay. The point is, after you've finished all the categories, sit back and take a good look at your family tree. What did you learn? How does that impact you? Try to identify ANY feelings it may bring up for you. And then sit with the feeling. Don't change your mental radio station: stay with the feelings. If it brings up disbelief or sadness or understanding and relief, sit with it. Take a pause and feel that feeling. Shame? Embarrassment? Confusion? If it brings up nothing, is that the same as numb? Are you feeling numb? Dead?

Suggestion 5:
Write a Letter to Each of Your Parents or Primary Caregivers

This could be your mom and dad, your stepparents, grandparents, aunts, uncles, birth parents, adoptive parents, older siblings, a nanny, etc. Each of the letters you write — and this is the most important part — must be written WITHOUT THE INTENTION OF SENDING. Let me say that again: each of the letters you write, DO NOT SEND. This is for two reasons. First of all, you don't have to worry about language. You can say f-you every other word if you like. You don't have to worry about grammar. You don't have to worry about editing. You don't have to worry about hurting someone's feelings. You can write unedited.

Secondly, you are not writing this letter for them. You are writing it for you. For *your* recovery. This is not about trying to get them to get it — it's about trying to get you to get it. Leave them out of the equation at this point. Writing down your gut-honest, most vulnerable feelings is healing and clarifying. SENDING the letter, is not. You only open up your most vulnerable self to a potentially unsafe person with an unsafe response. Your parent(s) may never get it. What's important is that you get it. It's your life — invest your energy in *your* getting it and not *their* getting it.

Being raised with an alcoholic father, I decided to go to ACA meetings (Adult Children of Alcoholics twelve-step meetings) as part of my emotional recovery work. I usually had a two-year-old tantrum with myself the whole way to the meeting, "Why do *I* have to go? *I* wasn't the alcoholic! Why do *I* have to sit in these stupid meetings and use up MY time? This isn't fair! Why isn't HE the one taking up HIS time doing this? Why do *I* have to do this?!" Then one day it occurred to me that the answer to the "Why me?" question was: because it's *my* life. I'm the one that's broken — I didn't cause it, but I got broken nonetheless. *I* need to do the work because *I* need to heal because *I* deserve to be happy. Yes, my father was broken, too, but my energies needed to go into fixing me. HIS energies needed to go into fixing HIM.

So it is with you. Don't send the letters you write. Concentrate on fixing YOU. You don't need your parent(s) to get it for you to heal. You do need yourself to get it.

Write a letter to each of your primary caregivers. Even if you had an absent, unavailable parent, write to him/her. Even if your parent is dead, write to him/her. I do not recommend that you write more than one letter a day. Write one, take a couple of days off, then write the next. You may have more than two letters to write. I had four: one each to my mother and father and then one each to my stepmother and step-father. I wrote to my stepparents because they were both in my life since I was four years old and both impacted me greatly. So, first figure out who you need to write.

In each letter, write what it was like to have them as a parent/caregiver. Tell them what you liked and what you didn't like. Tell them what you wished would have been different. Tell them what you needed from them that you didn't get. Be general and be specific. Tell them in general what didn't work well, and give them specific examples. Tell them how their parenting impacted you. Tell them the ramifications of their parenting. Tell them your anger. Tell them your hurt. Focus on the deficits — not what went right. Remember, you don't have to heal what went right — you have to heal the deficits. This isn't a letter saying thank you, dad, for all that you did. It's a letter saying, dad, why didn't you hold me? Why did you yell so much? Didn't you know it scared me? It's not a letter saying mom you were great. It's a letter saying, mom, why were you such a victim? Why didn't you stand up for yourself? Remember back to little you. Ten years old. Eight years old. Six years old. Tell them what it was like to have them as a parent in third grade, seventh grade, etc.

In the letter, because you are not going to send it, you can be hard on them, disrespectful, ugly towards them. You can say things you wished you could have said to them growing up. You can say things that you wish you had the nerve or opportunity to now. You can be brutally honest.

At the end of each letter, sit with your feelings. Identify how the writing impacted you. Sit. Do nothing. Feel any feelings you might be having. Then, burn the letter. Try to identify what you are feeling as you watch it burn.

Suggestion 6:
 Go To The Grave

If your parent is dead, or grandparent who raised you, or both parents, go to the grave and "chat." You can take the letter you've written in suggestion five and read it to them. Or just tell them about what it said. You can tell them what it's like for you that they are dead. You may have multiple conflicting feelings about their being dead. That's what separates us from other animals. We can have intense opposite feelings at the same time. You may feel glad your father's dead and immensely sad at the same moment. You may feel anger, hatred, bitterness, and yet long to see him one last time just to give him a hug and tell him you love him. You may feel abandoned, lonely. The goal is, of course, to feel SOMETHING. Get to your tears if you can. Emotionally connect with that lost parent/caregiver if you can. Sit on the grave. Stand on the grave. Kick the grave. Talk to the person buried there. Complain to, YELL at. Spend time with him or her. Tell them what you need them to know. Tell them how much you miss them. Tell them your struggles. Tell them about your children.

Then, say goodbye. Breathe. And feel whatever it is you're feeling. Let yourself feel.

Suggestion 7:
Observe Children

Go to the zoo. Go to a park. Go to a toy store. Go to the YMCA on a Saturday morning and watch the little league games. Notice two things. First of all, how connected they are to their feelings. Notice how intensely they feel and know you were like that as a child, too. Pretend that you are them doing whatever they are doing. Note the children who are already shutting down emotionally. Note the ones who are still fully alive.

Secondly, notice how old the children are. You can just guess or ask the parent if you'd like. Really soak in their ages and remember back when you were their ages: 5, 3, 8, 15, 12. Sometimes when I ask my clients to do this exercise, they are stunned by how small a child is at a given age. Connect back to when significant events happened in your life. If your parents divorced when you were 4, look for a 4 year old, then say to yourself, "That's how big I was when dad left." Or if you were working by age 12, find a 12 year old. "That's how old I was when I started working and had to take care of my younger sister." I had a client who built his own motorcycle from a kit when he was 8 years old. That's pretty amazing when you find an 8 year old and take a good look at how big 8 is. I worked with another man whose father wanted him to be a professional baseball player. His father built him a batting cage when he was six. Then 2-3 hour "practices" started each day, 6-7 days a week. (His is an example of emotional incest: where the child is to meet the need of the parent.) When my client observed a 6 year old boy he began to weep. He said, "I was so little. That's when my dad took over my life. I was SO little." He never became a professional ball player. He did have a lot of bitterness over a lost childhood. He also found every woman he dated "controlling." What a surprise.

Observe children. Try to connect with your own childhood experiences at that age. Observe what you're feeling. Give yourself permission to feel it.

Suggestion 8:
Do a New Warrior Weekend

The New Warrior Training Adventure is part of The Mankind Project, an international movement to help men. It is a weekend spent with a group of men working to get reconnected to their emotions and their personal power. It is a weekend which begins with a group of men all as apprehensive about the idea as you are. It's a group of men who think, "What am I doing here?" the same as you will. That's NORMAL. Feel the fear and do it anyway. You will be working with experienced staff who will help you. You are going there to learn something new. Don't expect yourself to know how to do the activities ahead of time. Give yourself some space to learn. The only requirement for a successful weekend is willingness, openness. It will stretch your comfort zone limits which, of course, is never comfortable in the beginning, but very rewarding once it's done.

In general, men I ask to do a New Warrior weekend come back more alive. They are more connected to their feelings and their "life force." They are more comfortable with themselves. They report being glad they went. Give it a go. It's only one weekend of your life. What have you got to lose — besides your fear? I highly recommend this. IF YOU FOLLOW THROUGH WITH NO OTHER SUGGESTION IN THIS BOOK, DO THIS. Since this is an international organization, they can most readily be found via their website: www.newwarrior.com.

Suggestion 9:
Talk To Your Parent Directly

This is not a one-time event. It will be a series of conversations where you practice speaking the truth and getting more and more authentic. You can open the conversation by asking your parent to talk about his or her childhood. Ask about your grandparents' childhoods. Gather information. This may be the end of your first conversation.

Let it rest a few days. Then go back and open more conversation, perhaps starting to talk to him/her about your own childhood. I don't know you, so I don't know what it is that would be helpful for you to say to your parent/s. But you do. You have a good brain and can figure it out.

When I started my own recovery work I picked my safest parent to begin to have real conversations with, my mother. I told her that I was learning about myself and our family. I told her I believed my father was an alcoholic. She was with me so far. Then I told her I thought our family had been dysfunctional in a lot of ways. That's when I lost her. She got defensive and told me I was wrong. She got hurt. She got angry. I remember her saying, "Why are you trying to hurt me?" and my reply, "Mom, I'm not trying to hurt you — I'm trying to TALK to you." She defended and defended. She cried. I got frustrated. I ended our maybe five minute conversation with, "If we were such a highly functional family, how come all of your kids are so screwed up?"

It didn't go well, I'd say. In fact, it went poorly. But it was the beginning. Of cutting through denial systems, of getting more "real" with each other. Our next conversation she defended her children vehemently; I pointed out all of our problems. For Christmas that year I sent her and my stepfather a series of 10 video tapes by John Bradshaw called *Bradshaw on the Family* (you may order these tapes by calling 1-800-6Bradshaw). They watched them. We talked some more. I explained I wasn't trying to blame them. We talked some more. It wasn't easy. Some of the conversations went better than others. They began to look at their own histories. It took us a couple of years to get to the point where we could consistently speak the truth to each other — not the sugar-coated version — and discuss hurts of the past. It wasn't easy, but it was worth it. We have an open, authentic relationship today.

I was lucky. I had two parents who got real with me. It was only through *my* pushing, however, that it happened. It would have never been initiated by them. You have to be the one pushing if you want things to be authentic between you and your parent. It won't come from your parent. You have to be the initiator and be tenacious. You have to be the one who keeps coming back with healthy behavior whether or not they are able to. If one of them cuts you off, you can respond in a healthy way. Tell them it feels like they are trying to cut you off and that you are not signing up for that. Call them. Continue to express yourself honestly. You can — and must — have healthy behavior whether or not they are able to. Your parents' generation had even less permission to have their feelings and authentic relationships than your generation. So when you are afraid, remember it feels scary to them, too. Remember, too, that scary is just a feeling.

Sometimes The Answer Is Never

With some parents, you will never be able to have an open, honest relationship. It depends on how damaged they were as children. The most severe damage happens between birth and age two when a child is not able to bond with a caregiver. We call that in psychological terms, an attachment disorder. This leads to sociopathology and narcissistic personality disorders.

In both of these cases, the person is unable to even comprehend that there is any experience besides his/her own. This person does not have empathy. This person does not hurt when hurting you. He (or she) is so very disconnected from his feelings, that he isn't even remotely aware of your pain. This person is severely wounded and is not able to hear what you are saying because, in essence, your experience doesn't really exist to him. Common characteristics of a person who was unbonded as a child are: lack of empathy, must be seen as the "hero," often feels a victim, seems overly concerned about his mother, and has an abundance of charm. These people are absolutely charming. They can charm anyone into anything. They are able to make outrageous requests because they don't know they are inappropriate. They might know it intellectually, but not emotionally. In Joseph Wambaugh's 1970's book, *The Onion Field*, the author interviews one of the cop killers. He asks the killer what he thinks about the cop's wife and two children that were left behind. His answer, "Nothing."

Thus is sociopathology. No remorse, no empathy, no emotional connection.

However, not all sociopaths and narcissistic personality disorders are killers. Most are not. Most walk among us daily, hold down jobs, make lots of money, do hero things. But they have no genuine empathy. They can't "get" the "other" experience, because it just doesn't exist for them. They feel hurt and victimized and often angry. They can be really mean because they don't connect to how that might feel to you. And the next minute, they can be really charming — if they want something.

If you have a parent who fits into this extremely damaged profile, you can forget about their ever "getting" it. They will not. No matter how good you are, how successful you are, how wonderful you are. No matter how directly you speak to them or how good you get at speaking the truth. They will NEVER get it. Most people in the psychology field believe that if we do not get a child to bond at a deep level with someone by age eight, we have lost them. We can never recover them and teach them empathy. Never. I have read of a very few cases where an unbonded child has been able to bond as late as age ten. One case of an 11 year old, one case of a 12 year old. People who were truly unbonded as children do not recover at age 40 or 50 or 60. The killer in The Onion Field, no matter how many New Warrior weekends he attends, no matter how much therapy he has, no matter how much love and acceptance he receives, will not heal at an emotional level. Ever. You may have a parent like that.

I did. As I mentioned earlier, my father was a sociopath. Before I came to this awareness, I tried for years so desperately to get him to get it. Then one day when I said to him, "Someday I'd like to talk to you honestly about what it was like to have you as a dad growing up," he became enraged and started screaming, "I was a GREAT father! I was the best G—Damned father there was! I was a superb father! If your grandmother were alive she would tell you what a great father I was . . ." etc. It was at that moment I realized, "He will never be any more honest than this." I realized, because of his damage, he COULDN'T be. No matter how many times I pointed out concrete evidence of his extreme abuse to me and my brother — and his inappropriate behavior that was so out there, he could never get it. So, even in his defended, puffed up, rageful state, I was able to more clearly self-define. You can, too. The point is, talking to your parent is worth doing. Even if your parent doesn't ever get it, doesn't ever get honest with you, doesn't ever get honest with himself, doesn't ever get authentic — you will.

So, talk to your parent(s) directly. Try to talk about the hard stuff. Practice speaking the truth — even when they resist hearing it. Be as kind as you can be. Again, this isn't about blaming them. It's about trying to cut through denial systems and getting to your authentic self. It's about being able to look at the hurtful things of the past, take ownership of them, and then reconnect to your feelings about them. Again, try to be kind to your parents in the process. It's hard for them, too. It's new information, new territory for them, too.

Suggestion 10:
   Think About Your Own Children

Have you been a good father? Being a good father means loving your children in such a way that deep down in their souls they know they are loved and valued by you. Do your kids know that? It means being dependable. Have you been dependable? It means being and acting like an adult. Do your kids have a sense of security and a feeling that they can count on you? Have you role modeled a successful, happy, loving relationship with a partner? It's your job to teach them (through example) how to have a successful, meaningful relationship. Are you doing that? How volatile are you? Do your children feel safe around you? Are you happy? Have you taught them to be happy beyond material possessions? When you think about the sacredness of your children and how important you are in each of their lives, are you being a good father?

Rank yourself on a scale of 1 to 10, 1 being low and 10 being high. If you're on the lower half of the scale, it's probably because you didn't have a good role model to teach you how to be a good father. Feel any feelings you may have about this. Be gentle with yourself. This suggestion is not about beating yourself up. It's about understanding. It's about trying to connect to the part of yourself that, for whatever reason, you got cut off from: your feeling self. Sometimes thoughts of our own children can get us there.

Suggestion 11:
  Go To Sappy Movies

I'm not talking about love stories — although a love story may work. I'm talking about movies with some depth. Substantive. Emotional. Choose movies that might hit a nerve for you. *Field of Dreams. A Beautiful Mind. I am Sam. The Green Mile. The Sixth Sense. Rudy. As Good As It Gets. Pearl Harbor.* Look for the emotional growth of the characters. Look for the emotional struggle. Try to feel what the main character might be feeling. See if you can emotionally "connect" into the story.

I have known numerous men who have used this technique as their vehicle to get to their feelings. It may work for you. It may not. Try it and see. Do not stuff in your emotions if they begin to surface. If you're at the theatre, it's dark. Nobody knows you there. Let yourself cry. If you're at home, turn off the lights. It's dark. Let yourself cry.

Suggestion 12:
  Think About Your Parents' Marriage

Do you think they had a good marriage? Would you want it? Why or why not? What parts of the marriage seemed to work and what parts do you in no way want in your own significant relationship? You may be surprised to find that how you interact with your spouse is not too different than how your parents interacted. So? So, do you want it to be that way? How do you need to change to change the system?

Suggestion 13:
  Eye Contact

This may relate to you. It may not. If you are a person who has difficulty making and maintaining eye contact with people, I encourage you to practice changing that. Take the next week or two and FORCE yourself to look people in the eye. First, when they are talking to you and then second, when you are talking to them. Research shows people tend to maintain eye contact longer when they are listening than when they are speaking. So, give yourself some grace on the speaking part. Look at the person as much as you can. It won't be 100 percent. We're not trying for 100 percent. We're trying for *increasing* the amount of eye contact you can tolerate. If you're starting at 0 percent and get to 20%, that's great. Look people directly in the eye. As you are doing this, try to take note of any feelings you might be having. If this has been a problem for you and you practice long enough, you should arrive at a point of feeling increased power and confidence. It may be scary at first, anxiety producing, painful, shameful, feel odd, feel impossible. You might be aware of feeling small, like a child. Keep practicing.

FORCE yourself to make and maintain eye contact. Note what you're feeling. And keep practicing everyday for 1–2 weeks.

Suggestion 14:
  Practice One Sentence Confrontations

One sentence confrontations are a way of speaking your truth directly without getting into an argument. I find so many, many men who "hate confrontations." They will do ANYTHING to avoid a confrontation, most notably saying yes to something they really want to say no to. When I ask them to describe a confrontation, they inevitably describe an awful interaction that gets out of control and ends in a huge argument or a hurricane.

The one sentence confrontation is a way to look at confrontation differently. First of all, it's not big. It's small. It's one sentence, maybe two, with no room left open for discussion. You are not trying to discuss the issue. You are merely making a statement about it. One sentence, maybe two. You do not want to know the other person's take on things. The one sentence confrontation involves carefully selecting words that number one, speak your truth, and number two, are intended to be thought-provoking. They cut to the chase and leave no room for discussion. Once you have said your one sentence confrontation, you simply go on to the next beat. For example: "That was rude. So anyway, let's go get some lunch." Or, "You seem to be coming from such a place of fear. I hope to make things safer for you. Anyway, I also wanted to talk to you about the kids' soccer schedules. I need to get those in my calendar." Or, "Well, THAT hurt my feelings. Anyway, blah, blah, blah," and onto the next subject.

Personally I love one sentence confrontations. I love to challenge myself to see how effective I can be in one sentence. It's fun. I do think they are an art form, too. The more you practice them, the better you get at them. Like learning to play the piano, you will not be good at them at first. You'll be *lousy*. Keep practicing.

Eventually you will learn to add humor to them where it increases your effectiveness and leave humor out where it decreases your effectiveness. I love one sentence confrontations because they really help you stop playing "ping pong" with your partner (p. 69). One sentence confrontations can help you listen differently, too. Hear what your partner is saying and then formulate a summary as to how it impacts you. You have one sentence, two max. This is not a reactionary technique. It is a very proactive and deliberate technique. It's a lot like poetry. You get very few words to make an important point. Choose your words with care. This is not about flinging out smart aleck one-liners, either. If you only get one or two sentences, don't waste them on smart aleck remarks.

Remember, your goal is to be effective, not a jerk. You are not trying to hurt your partner with a one sentence confrontation. You are trying to number one, speak your truth, and number two, be thought-provoking.

An Example

When my oldest son, Scott, was 5, he loved Lego sets. So my father, ever needing to be the hero, started buying him Lego sets. And Lego sets. And Lego sets. It became clear to my husband and me that this was not good for our son. So I asked my father to stop buying Scott Lego sets because too much was not good for him. I told him our little guy still had three boxes he hadn't even built yet.

The next day, as my son and I were outside, my father drove up, honked his horn, and gestured for Scott to come to the car. He then gave him a huge Toys "R" Us bag filled with two $150 Lego sets along with these words, "Tell your mother these are not your toys. Tell her they are MY toys, and I said you could build them for me." To me he waved and shouted, "Don't be angry!" as he drove away laughing.

Of course I was angry, and after quelling my internal volcanic eruption, I thought to myself, "I need a one sentence confrontation." After much thought I decided on these words and said them to my father — in front of my son — the next time I saw him: "Dad, was I not clear to you that we did not want you to buy Scott any more Lego sets?" to which he laughed and said, "Oh, yeah, you were clear. I just ignored you." Then — here is the one sentence confrontation said looking him directly in the eye — "You said not to be angry at you and actually, Dad, I mostly felt disrespected. I'm sorry you were not able to demonstrate respect for my parenting choices." Now, I knew my father needed to be seen as the hero by my son. He retorted, "I respect your parenting choices!" to which I responded, "Enough said. Boys, let's get the table set." I then got up and helped set the table. I was not opening up the topic for discussion or debate. I spoke my truth. I left him to think about it. That is a one sentence confrontation. The postscript is that my father didn't buy any more Lego sets.

Now, one sentence confrontations are not always effective, but they often are. Practice, practice, practice them, and see how effective you can get.

Suggestion 15:
Identify What Is Fun For You and Do It

Sometimes emotionally unavailable men have lost contact with their playful self. The child within. The joyful, free, laughing, fun self. At other times, emotionally unavailable men use this part of themselves to avoid feeling anything. Life's a party. They play and play and play and play. If you are in the latter group, this suggestion is not for you. If you are in the former group, read on.

When you ask yourself when was the last time I really had fun — unadulterated, non-chemically induced, fun — what is your answer? If you can't even remember when the last time was, then chances are you need to make this suggestion a top priority. First of all, identify what you like to do for fun. Make a list. What is fun to you? Going to the movies? Eating out? Building things? Cooking? Having people over? Playing cards? Golfing? Reading? Singing? Going to concerts? Going to the ball game? I suggest that you make sure there is something physical on your list: dancing, jet skiing, rollerblading, bowling, snow skiing, having sex, playing baseball, running a 5K, hiking, scuba diving, etc. Then, add something to your list that you've often thought about doing but never did: skydiving, flying in a hot air balloon, visiting all 50 states, climbing a mountain, bicycling 100 miles, driving a stock car in a race, taking trumpet lessons, taking a photography class, etc.

After your list is done, pick one thing and do it. Then evaluate it on a "fun scale." On a scale of 1 to 10, how fun was it? Then, go on to another thing on your list, and do that, etc., until you've done everything on your list at least once. After you've finished your list — or at least gotten close to finishing, go back and start doing more of the items that ranked high on your fun scale. My sister, who is wonderfully wise and is a personal trainer, has a sign posted in her gym: figure out what feels good to you and do it often.

A word of warning, however. This exercise sometimes brings up grief for people. They are struck with the sadness of lost time, so many years without joy. They are reminded of shame: sometimes feeling good feels bad because they were shamed as children for playing. This may happen to you. That's okay. You can celebrate reconnecting with your feelings. Let yourself grieve — and continue to do things on your list. I promise you there will come a time when having fun feels good. You deserve that.

Suggestion 16:
Go To a Twelve-Step Meeting

There are lots of twelve-step meetings, AA (Alcoholics Anonymous) being the most well known. The twelve-step meeting I most recommend, however — if there is no addiction involved — is Adult Children of Alcoholics. The meetings are free. They will help you take responsibility for your life and your feelings, plus self-define. I recommend you attend the same meeting six times to see if it fits for you. I also recommend that you go to a "mixed" meeting. That is, a meeting with both men and women in it. Let's face it, women have had more permission to have their feelings. You want to make sure and be exposed to that. You can get a list of Adult Children meetings by calling Al-Anon (listed in the business white pages) and asking for AC meetings. If you are a nonsmoker, I suggest asking for a nonsmoking meeting.

If you have an addiction, I recommend that you start with the twelve-step meeting that is specifically designed for your addiction. AA for drinking issues, CA for cocaine issues, SAA for sexual addiction issues, OA for overeating issues, GA for gambling problems, and NA, Narcotics Anonymous, for drug involvement. First get your addiction cleaned up and then you will be ready to do the deeper level work. The deeper level stuff is what brought you to the addiction in the first place. I see addiction as the symptom, and usually, unresolved family of origin issues as the problem. So, first get rid of the symptom, and then you will be clear to address the problem.

Suggestion 17:
Turn Off The TV For A Week

This is a concrete, simple exercise. Literally, turn off the TV for one week. If TV is not your particular "escape," then turn off your particular "escape" for one week. The important thing is to become aware of how this impacts you. Does it create anxiety for you? Serenity? Both? Try to label what you're feeling.

Suggestion 18:
Empty Chair Role Play

I suggest taking two chairs and facing them toward each other. You sit in one of the chairs and, in your imagination, "place" one of your parents in the other. Now, close your eyes and imagine yourself as a young boy. It doesn't matter how old you see yourself as long as you are a child. Get a good grasp on your age. Are you in elementary school, junior high, or high school? Try to get a good visual picture of yourself. What are you wearing? Now, from that age, open your eyes and address each of your parents (or caregivers). Tell them, one at a time, what it is you need from them.

For example, to your dad you might say: I need you to be home more. I need you to be nice to mom. I need you to coach my little league team and come to my games. I need you to be involved in my life. I need you to listen to me. I need you to stop drinking. I need you to be normal. I need you to do special things with me. I need you to stop yelling.

And so forth. Then talk to your mom. Tell her, from your little boy point of view, what you need from her. Speak in the present tense. Try to get to your tears, get to your pain, get to your loss.

Next, close your eyes and allow yourself to change into the age you are today. Place your wife/partner/girlfriend in the empty chair and tell her what you need from her. Let yourself feel.

Suggestion 19:
  Stop Lying To Yourself

If you haven't seen the movie, *Liar, Liar*, with Jim Carey, it's a good one to rent. In it, Jim Carey is magically prevented from telling any lies — even tiny ones — for 24 hours. Hilarity follows. I often think about that movie and give my clients the same 24-hour challenge. No lies. Not even to yourself. Actually, this is the crux of all recovery: learning to tell the truth.

In my own recovery I went to an Adult Children of Alcoholics meeting and the topic was Telling the Truth. I relaxed in my chair thinking, *Oh, this really doesn't pertain to me. I tell the truth. I'm honest. I don't lie.* But, as I sat there listening to others speak on all the variations of this theme, I began to squirm a little. Maybe it did pertain to me just a bit. By the end of the meeting I sat there stunned realizing I had a major problem with honesty. That my whole life was actually built on lies. Now, I wasn't the kind of person that would tell you I didn't do something that I did. But I was the kind of person that if you didn't ask me, I might not tell you. Which I know now is dishonest. In fact, if there is ANY intention of deceiving or misleading — even through omission — it's dishonest. Do you do that?

The second way I was dishonest, I discovered at that meeting, was that I didn't tell MYSELF the truth. I constantly told myself things about myself that weren't true: that I wasn't smart enough, pretty enough, good enough; that I was a victim and there was nothing I could do about the way things were. Do you do that? Do you tell yourself lies about yourself? These lies, of course, are rooted in family of origin messages to us as children. They are, nonetheless, not true. You ARE good enough, smart enough, nice looking enough. You are not a less than. You are not a second class citizen. Stop acting like one. You are not a victim. You have choices. Figure out what they are and take some action. Do something to change your situation if you're not happy. Have boundaries. Be proactive.

Take the 24-hour challenge. No lies. Not to yourself. Not to others. That means you are going to have to examine every word that comes out of your mouth for a full day. You are going to have to stay consciously connected to your thoughts for a full day. This exercise is not to be taken lightly. Do it deliberately. Increase your consciousness about what you say to yourself and what you say to others for 24 hours. I wish you well and good luck. This is a difficult exercise if done correctly.

Suggestion 20:
Do One Thing A Day To Care For Your Partner

For the next week, Sunday to Sunday, do one thing a day that will make your relationship better. It has to be something you do on purpose, not something you look back on at the end of the day and say, "Well, I did that and that was nice." Something above and beyond the call of duty. Something big. Each day for 7 days. Note how it feels to give and to make someone happy. Note how it feels to receive praise and thank yous.

P.S. If you are not in a relationship with a partner right now, do this exercise with 7 different people. They need to be people you know: people at work, your family, your friends. Do something noticeable to take care of people throughout the week. This doesn't mean sitting down and writing a check to support a favorite charity of yours. It needs to be much more personal than that. A one on one interaction. Also, if you have been the hero child in your family, you must do these caring things anonymously. If you are found out, you have not done the exercise well. One of my clients, who was not the hero child in his family, decided to do this exercise picking people he couldn't stand. He chose one particularly obnoxious woman at work to begin with. He bought her a small gift, wrapped it, and even gave her a hug when he presented it to her. He gave it to her privately and told her that the gift was to cheer her up, because he wanted her to have more happiness in her life. Tears swelled in her eyes — and his.

Suggestion 21:
  Pray, Sit With Nature, Meditate

Prayer is hard for a lot of people. You may be one of them. Especially if you have no concept of God or a Higher power that makes sense to you. In that case, spend time in silent meditation. Try to clear thought from your brain and sit with a blank slate. The most important thing is to take time to be quiet and that in this quiet time you focus on reconnecting with your feelings. In prayer, where you are comfortable with the concept of a Higher power, you might say, "Dear God, help me reconnect to my feeling self. I need help. It doesn't make sense to me. I turn this request over to you, Lord." In meditation, where you are not comfortable with the concept of a Higher power, you might say, "I allow myself to reconnect with my feelings again. I allow myself to be whole."

P.S. If you are in a struggle with yourself about church and God and spirituality, etc., I personally love the Unitarian Universalist Church. These churches offer a space for you to safely question everything without judgment. They offer a respectful space for you as you try to figure out what you do believe and what you do not believe. They support the inherent worth and dignity of every human being: including you. They are listed in your phone book.

Suggestion 22:
  Look For ADD

This may sound odd, but it's important to rule out. There are mountains of information on ADD (Attention Deficit Disorder) and here I will only skim the very, very surface of it. Until the 1990's, it was believed that children with ADD outgrew it. Now we know that some children seem to outgrow it while most do not. It is now an adult diagnosis as well as a childhood diagnosis.

There are two forms of ADD: with and without hyperactivity. If a person has ADHD, it usually shows. He talks fast, he skips around from topic to topic, he moves around in his seat, he seems disorganized and hyper. If a person has ADD without the hyperactivity, that can — and does — often go undiagnosed. This person looks out the window and daydreams, doesn't finish projects, is a financial disaster, doesn't do a lot of future planning, works slowly and doesn't seem to get much work done in the allotted time, has piles and piles of papers he's "going to get to," and often doesn't follow through on his word — because, quite frankly, he forgets to. He appears, without diagnosis and treatment, to be irresponsible, unreliable, chaotic, and in a perpetual state of being overwhelmed.

People with ADD or ADHD have, really, not an attention *deficit*, but an attention *plethora*. It's as if they have 12 radio stations blaring inside their heads at the same time with their attention skipping from one to another to another and back again. If this sounds like you at all, it may be part of an explanation of why you appear emotionally unavailable. People with ADD/ADHD often don't stay on their feelings long enough to identify them, let alone express them.

If you relate to these paragraphs, I highly recommend your reading (and your partner reading) *Driven to Distraction* by Dr. Edward Hallowell and Dr. John Ratey. This book is also on tape if that is easier for you. It is my favorite book on the market about ADD because it is written by two people who have ADD. Therefore, it isn't just about the theory of ADD, it's about actually living with it. I highly recommend, too, that you be evaluated by a competent clinician to determine whether or not ADD/ADHD is present. Because if it is, and it's diagnosed and treated, your life, and your relationship, can dramatically — DRAMATICALLY — improve.

P.S. I have no formal research to back up what I'm about to say, but I have queried every person I have met with ADD/ADHD or with a child with ADD/ADHD, whether there was raging in the house during that person's formative years of 0-3. The answer, invariable, has been yes. Perhaps raging disturbs how the child's brain development solidifies. I would be interested in seeing research done in this area that would either support or refute this informal query of mine. If you have ADD, was there raging in your home?

Suggestion 23:
  Ask Your Partner For A List

Ask your partner to write down a list of things you've done that hurt her. Don't let her tell you verbally. Next, study the list. After reading each item, ask yourself, did someone treat me that way? Who? It might not have been treating you with the same behavior, but more likely, in the same way. For example: with disregard for your feelings, making you invisible, being verbally abusive, pointing out your faults, never being satisfied, giving you the message that you weren't important, being critical, etc.

Now, check in with yourself as far as your feelings. Are you surprised? Angry? Sad? Disturbed? Pensive? Numb?

P.S. You need to help your partner here. She needs to know her list did not fall into the black hole. You might show her the exercise you are doing. You might thank her for the list and explain that you are working on changing things for her. You might just validate her experience by saying, "You're right. I did do all those things. And I wish I had the chance to do it all over again. I would do it differently. That's what I'm working on now. *Changing* it."

And you ARE. If you are doing this exercise, you ARE working on changing it.

Suggestion 24:
  Visualization

If you had a particularly abusive or violent childhood, this exercise is essential. Since this needs to be done with your eyes closed, you'll have to read this through several times before beginning.

Close your eyes. Go back in time. See yourself as a twenty year old. Eighteen year old. Fourteen year old. Ten year old. Eight year old. Then five or six. Don't worry about exact ages. Just try to see yourself young, about the age of early elementary school. See yourself doing something. What are you doing? Playing? Hiding? Laughing? Crying? Are you scared? Of what? Now hold that image in your head as you add yourself (at your present age) into the picture. Pretend there's a magic portal you can step through to go back and meet your young self.

Greet him gently. Tell him who you are. Tell him you are going to take him out of his crazy home life and bring him back to live with you. Promise him that you'll keep him safe. Promise him that you'll love him, and value him, and take care of him. Take his hand gently and walk to the portal. Before you go through the portal, though, turn around and face your caregivers. Tell them, "He's coming with me now. You're not allowed to hurt him anymore." Then turn and walk through the portal with your little boy.

This concept of your adult self taking care of your wounded child self is very important. You didn't have good parenting, and so now, you have to parent yourself. Do what you would do with a child: love him, protect him, help him, nurture him, give him a break, be kind to him. Love you, protect you, help you, nurture you, give yourself a break, be kind to you.

I have found for some people doing this visualization one time is enough. With others, they have to keep going back for their little self over and over again until finally they rescue him for good. Do the visualization as many times as you need to.

Suggestion 25:
Look For Emotional Incest

To understand emotional incest better, it might be helpful to re-read the section on page 77. After having done so, it's time to get honest with yourself about it. Were you the chosen child? Were you the favorite? Were you the hero child? Emotional incest can happen when the child is chosen in a negative way, too. For example, if you were the chosen scapegoat for the family, that is also emotional incest.

If you were the chosen child, positively or negatively, it's impor-tant to name it and claim it. To really take ownership of it. You have to know your dragon to fight it. Furthermore, it's important to acknowledge that, at an unconscious level, the emotional incest blocks your ability to fully connect with another person. Emotionally incested children grow up to be adults whose core belief is, "If I love and connect to another, I disappear." It's vital that you bring this out of your subconscious and into your conscious thinking.

It would be good to do some grieving around the years you've lost trying to hold onto yourself and trying to make space for yourself, and about how difficult relationships have been due to the emotional incest. It would be good to do some grieving around the disappearing you've done and the years of giving your power away because you didn't know how to have boundaries and had to choose avoidance due to the emotional incest. It would be good to get clear that it is a formidable force in your life and in your relationships, and to do some grieving around that.

Suggestion 26:
Have You Been A Good Husband?

Think about your wife — have you been a good husband? Have you been a good marital partner? What's a good marital partner anyway? Well, would you marry you?

Have you been true to your marriage vows? Have you been faithful? In both body and spirit? Have you loved and *honored* your wife? Have you cared for her in sickness and in health? I love that sentiment: have you cared for — taken care of — your wife in health? Is she able to recognize your caring? Does she experience you as a caring person towards her? Have you been financially responsible? Have you done your part?

Here's another simple test of assessment: is your wife happy? No, you are not responsible for *making* your wife happy, but if she is not happy, you probably need to adjust some things. If your wife is not happy, that's simply a barometer which says something's not working. For whatever reason, your love is not coming through. Do you know why? If not, ask her. She can tell you. Are you willing to change it to make things better?

If you go through this assessment process, get bluntly honest with yourself, and if you come up with no, I haven't been a good husband, I think it's important to sit with that information. Not to beat yourself up with it. Lord knows you've probably been beaten up enough about it. Just sit there with the realization and feel whatever you feel about it. It certainly can be humbling to break through a little piece of your denial system. To admit to yourself that no, I haven't been a good partner.

The other thing is not to despair. If you've been a lousy husband, there's no place to go but up. Your power to heal the marriage is vast.

Suggestion 27:
Identify and Write Down What Is Sacred to You

Sacred is something that is so valuable to you that you would guard it, protect it, stand up for it. Some people think of it as holy. Identifying what is that valuable to you is closely tied to identifying your personal value system. This is important to do, for once you are clear on your values, how to get your behavior congruent with them becomes clear as well. Life gets a lot simpler if you are living congruent with your personal values. Of course, you can't do that unless you know what you value. So, what is sacred to you? What is sacred to me includes knowing myself and being true to myself, connecting with my husband on all levels, loving my children, having fun, and telling the truth. What about you? Write them down. Ponder them. Then identify and feel any feelings this might bring up for you.

Suggestion 28:
Go to Therapy

It's another thing to try. It's not a necessity, but it is an option. When I started my own recovery process 28 years ago, I went to a therapist for ten sessions. It was interesting, but I didn't feel I got much out of it. But I did. I was young and not quite ready to understand what he was offering. But it was going in. One, two, even five years after those ten hours, his words began to come back to me and make sense at a deeper level. Even now, 28 years later, having fully integrated those sessions into how I live my life, I am amazed at how powerful those mere ten hours were and how often I think of them.

It's an option I feel is worth trying. I think of going to a therapist like going to a medical doctor. If you had pneumonia or cancer or a broken bone, would you go to a doctor? Would you listen to what he or she had to say about how to get better? It's the same with mental health. If you are disconnected from your feelings and have mental pneumonia, it's okay to go to someone who is an expert in that field to listen to what he or she has to say about how to get better. And, as with choosing a doctor, make sure you're not going to a quack. Choose carefully. Reread page 92 on this topic.

Now it's time to go back and do these exercises. It's nice you read them, but you have to DO them to benefit from them.

Chapter 9

Living in Personal Integrity: Freedom

This is the chapter where the rubber hits the road. This is the chapter where you move from talking the talk to walking the walk. Talking the talk is not enough. You must commit to actually *doing* the work: to actually *changing*. Growing up. Living in personal integrity. You can do it.

I remember how frightened I was about childbirth a week before my first son was born. What if I died? I was relaying my fears to a friend of mine who was a nurse at the hospital where I was working. She looked at me in disbelief and with irritation in her voice said, "For God's sake, Patti, women have babies in the rice fields in China. They squat down, have their baby, get up, and start working again. Millions of women have had millions of babies. You will, too. Get over it." Then she huffed away and I sat there stunned. I had expected reassurance — not a slap in the face. Yet a slap in the face was exactly what I needed. A good dose of reality to help me realize that, "Yes, I am just like other people. Other people have done this for years and so will I."

That's what I say to you. So will you. There are haves and have nots in the world and for the most part there is only one difference between the two: personal integrity. The haves have learned how to tell themselves the truth, how to consciously self-define, and how to be true to themselves. And so can you.

Telling Yourself the Truth

You are good enough. You are capable. You are competent. You can figure things out. If you are telling yourself anything different, you are lying to yourself. You can't lie to yourself and live in personal integrity. Tell yourself the truth. You may have done a lot of crappy things in your life, but that doesn't change the fact that you are good enough, you are capable, you are competent, and you can figure things out. It just means that you've been acting out from a self-image that you carry around that isn't accurate. If the picture of yourself you carry around is "I'm not good enough," you will keep screwing up. If the picture of yourself changes to "I am good enough, I can figure this out, I am a nice person, I am capable and competent," you will stop screwing up. Now, no one's perfect and that is not the goal. Give yourself grace when you do screw up. However, the point is, the self-image you tote around with you will determine how often screw-ups happen.

The truth is there are no extraordinary people in this world. There are only ordinary people — like you, like me — who do extraordinary things. There are only ordinary people with red blood, taking in oxygen, fighting fatigue, looking at their faces in the mirror searching for lines, who hunger and thirst for happiness and acceptance just like you. Afraid. And they have DECIDED not to let those fears run their lives.

Live Life Even Though You Are Afraid

Mayor Rudy Giuliani was *Time* Magazine's 2001 Person of the Year. In *Time's* article about him, Giuliani says the last conversation he had with his father before he died of prostate cancer, "was about courage and fear. I said to him, 'Were you ever afraid of anything?' He said to me, 'Always.' He said, 'Courage is being afraid but then doing what you have to do anyway.'" Later in the article, Giuliani speaks of taking his 12-year-old daughter, Caroline, on a tour of Ground Zero. "She wanted to see it," he says. "She was upset but not overwrought.

It's my job to do for my kids what my father did for me — try to help them figure out how to deal with fear. How to live life, even though you are afraid."

And that's the goal: to live life even though you are afraid. And to live it well. You are good enough. You are capable. You are competent. Don't let fear get in your way. Fight it off over and over again.

Tell yourself the truth: fear is just a feeling. It won't kill you. In the Buddhist faith there is a belief that says feelings are temporary. I like that and think it's true. You will only feel afraid until you do what you are afraid of. When you get on the other side of it and discover you lived, then you won't have the feeling of fear anymore. You'll have the feeling of relief. And power. And freedom. Eleanor Roosevelt once said, "You must do the thing you think you cannot do." That's facing fear.

What if you fail? You will. Many times. That's normal. What if you make a mistake? You will. Many times. That's normal. Keep trying. Ordinary people who do extraordinary things fail many, many, many times, but believe they are enough, are capable, are competent. Failure doesn't mean STOP. It means THINK. Figure it out. Dig. Get to a deeper level of self-honesty.

Reprogramming

Part of telling yourself the truth is learning to reprogram your self-talk. Your brain is a complex, incredible computer. It has been recording data from before you were born. Some of that data — I'd venture to say a good chunk of it — is inaccurate. This causes your computer to respond in skewed, limiting ways. If only there were a delete button. If only we could round up all the lies you were told about yourself and push the delete button and they'd be gone. Wouldn't that be great? Unfortunately, people don't come with delete buttons. Unfortunately, our reprogramming takes longer than a swift press of a key. Just imagine how many thousands and thousands of times you have told yourself self-limiting, dishonest statements, over the years. It's going to take time to counter those. That's okay. That's normal. But start today.

What does that mean? It means working to silence your self-critical voice and working to silence your fearful voice, and doing it over, and over, and over again. Remember your voice dialogue (page 48). Since our brains cannot hold two thoughts at the same moment, whenever a critical or fearful statement comes into your head, you must learn to battle it. Hire an internal "bouncer" or "bodyguard." A big brute of a guy who comes forward to protect you — from yourself. Whenever your critical voice or fearful voice starts messing with you, have your bouncer come forward and kick them out. Have your bouncer fire them. This, of course, is all done in your head. Have your bouncer make room for your new self who takes care of you, believes in you, your affirming self. Remember, you are reprogramming your computer. Taking out the stuff that works against you, typing in the new stuff that works for you.

Affirmations

Affirmations work FOR you. Affirmations are positive self-statements. They are poisonous to negative self-statements. They make the negatives shrivel up and die. They are essential for changing your self-talk and essential for walking the walk and affecting behavioral change. You must stop saying limiting statements to yourself and start saying encouraging things. Be your own personal trainer.

Some people find affirmations corny. They say how will this help me? I say, TRY IT. Right now you are brainwashing yourself to work against yourself. Try brainwashing yourself in your favor. Right now you are letting limiting, dishonest statements determine your behavior. Try working from supportive, life-expanding statements.

Some people find affirmations to be in direct conflict with self-honesty and personal integrity. They believe, deep in their souls, that they are not good enough, capable or competent. They feel like they are lying to themselves if they say anything positive about themselves.

You may be one of those people. That's fine. I was one of those people. The negative brainwashing I had received while growing up, especially from my father, was so thorough that I took it as TRUTH.

For you, I say, try to think of ANYTHING positive you can say to yourself that you can at least, at this point, half way believe. I chose the affirmation I started with, "I'm a good person," because I believed somewhere, under all the garbage and all the acting out, that there was a good person. So that's what I went with.

You'll have to find something that works for you, and then say it as your mantra 100 times a day. Keep in mind you are reprogramming ALL those negative self-statements that are in your computer. Repetition is good. In fact, it's essential. Once you are able to hold onto your first affirmation, add a second. Activate your "bouncer" when your critical voice pipes up — and it will — and replace it with a self-supportive statement. Continue this process until you can say: I am enough, I am capable, I am competent, I am lovable, I can do this, I can figure it out, I have a good brain, I am a good person, I am honest, I am valuable, without any back-talk from your critical voice. Don't be afraid to tell yourself the bad stuff, too. Just keep your critical voice in check while getting honest with yourself about the things in you and in your behavior you don't like and want to change. In twelve-step work, such as AA, this is called doing a fourth step. Taking a fearless personal inventory of yourself. That means telling the truth about the good stuff — like you are a good person, you are valuable, you are capable, etc. — and telling the truth about the bad stuff, too. Yes, I screwed up. Yes, I said I would do that and I didn't. Yes, I lied to you. Yes, I've been a lousy partner.

Whatever the bad stuff is, you don't have to shame yourself about it, you just have to get real about it. Admit it. To yourself. Call it like it is. Don't make it bigger than it is. Don't make it smaller. And keep your critical voice in check. You are not a bad person because you messed up. You are not a bad person even if you've messed up big time and lots of times. You probably have been lying to yourself at some level and it's time to change that. Make different decisions. Ones that are life-supporting of you. If you keep screwing up over and over and over again, you either have attention deficit disorder (ADD/ADHD), an addiction, or a self-image that is not accurate. By far, most of the men I work with have a self-image they are operating from that is not accurate. But, in getting truthful with yourself, make sure to rule out ADD, make sure to rule out addiction. If either is present, admit it, and get treatment for it.

Finances

For many people, being honest with yourself also means taking a look at your finances. If your finances are in order, skip this section. If they are not in order, take special note. I find that for many people, for whatever reason, effective finances seem directly proportional to level of self-honesty. This is *by no means* accurate across the board. There are many, many men who make boatloads of money and have a very low level of self-honesty. This section does not pertain to them. It pertains to the person who seems to always be struggling financially. The one who can't seem to quite make ends meet. If this is you, I want you to look for a deeper level of honesty explaining why this is.

You are not a victim. If you think you are financially, you are not being honest with yourself at any deep level. Are you in a low income job because you are afraid to challenge yourself and fail? or afraid to succeed? Do you lack good people skills? Do you need more education? If you are in business for yourself, do you keep your word to your customers? Do you stay in a low income job because it's safe? Are you used to poverty and don't trust people who make money?

You are capable, you are competent, so barring any undiagnosed and untreated ADD or addiction, you ought to be able to make money beyond a paycheck to paycheck level. How's your spending? Do you live within your means? Do you buy things on impulse? Can you really afford the things you buy? Are you using credit cards beyond your ability to pay them back? In other words, how responsible are you being with your money? Are you wasteful? Do you save for a rainy day at all? Do you have appropriate boundaries around money with others (i.e., your wife, kids, friends)? Do you know where you stand financially, or do you spend indiscriminately? That is, are you consciously connected to your spending? You are not a victim. If you are frequently in a financial bind, it's time to get more honest with yourself. As your self-honesty around finances increases, so, too, will your financial stability. If you lie to yourself about money, your financial instability will continue. It's a great barometer for some people and if your finances are not in order, it's probably a great barometer for you.

Self-Define: Question Your Truths

As children, we deify our parents. They know all. They have the answers. They are bigger than life. So naturally, what they tell us about ourselves and about how life is, we believe. And that's probably a good thing. As children, it gives us order, it gives us security, it provides answers. It helps us make sense out of a very complex world. We absorb what they say as Truths, however. The way life IS. Not to be questioned.

This section is about just the opposite. I want to encourage you to question all the Truths you were given. I want to encourage you to become aware of what you were taught and to question all those teachings to determine whether what you were taught rings true for you today. What I'm saying is, the Truths you were taught as a child might not be true at all! I'm also saying you must give yourself permission to discard things your parents taught you. You are an adult now. There is a whole new set of rules.

The rules of childhood include:

1. Our parents KNOW.

2. Our parents are teaching us correct information.

3. Our parents are authority figures. They make the rules. We have to listen to them or get punished.

4. This is the way it IS — don't question it. I never thought I would say to my kids, "Because I'm the mom, that's why," because I hated it when my mom said it to me. But I have said it . . .

5. Separation and individuation is not appropriate. We need our parents to survive. They, therefore, have a lot of power in our lives.

The rules of adulthood, however, are different:

1. You have choice — always.

2. You are allowed to question what your parents taught you. In fact, you need to in order to self-define. You are even allowed to question what your church taught you, or any other "authority" figure in your childhood.

3. You are allowed to discard information that was given to you that doesn't fit anymore.

4. Separation and individuation is a good thing. We do not need our parents to survive. We are allowed to — need to — develop our own personal truths and therefore, become our own personal authority.

5. You do not need your parent's permission to do this. (Or your wife's.)

Take What You Like and Leave the Rest

Self-definition, and personal power, come from painstakingly examining each and every Truth you were taught, and deciding whether to keep it as part of your own truth or to discard it. You probably can very quickly think of one thing your parents taught you as Truth that you don't believe anymore. What is it? My mother was taught that puppies come from the garden. Now, for us today, we can say that's pretty crazy. You're kidding, right? The reality is, no, I'm not kidding. She was taught that as a Truth, the way it IS. I was taught — point blank — that boys don't like smart girls. What were you taught that was equally absurd? My point is, if there was *one* thing that you were taught that was inaccurate, there were probably more. Start looking. Start examining everything. What you were taught about yourself, about life, about women, about work, about religion, about sex, about money, etc. Take what you like and leave the rest. This is self-definition.

Some of the Truths you were taught won't be so obvious. A lot of things we were taught weren't done so directly. We learned them through observation or we were told things in a round about way. Regardless of how we were taught our TRUTHS, we were, nonetheless, *taught* them. Now, as an adult, you need to examine those teachings and see if you *believe* them.

A simple way to do this is to take a piece of paper, choose any topic, and write down what you were taught about it. ANY topic. You were given a message about it and internalized it as TRUTH. Now is the time to decide whether the message you carry about it is one that works for you. For example, start with:

I am _____

Women are _____

Marriage is _____

Crying is _____

Pets are _____

God is _____

Men are_____

Write down the messages you carry. Do you believe them? You are probably acting in your life from the premise that you believe them, but DO you believe them? If you are acting from truths that you were taught as Truths, and yet you haven't really ever even questioned them or examined them, chances are you are not living in personal integrity. Why? Because you haven't done the work that is necessary to SELF-define. Instead, you are living from others' definitions of Truth. You must come to terms with what is true for you — which may be very different from what is true for your parents (or your wife) — in order to self-define and live in personal integrity.

What Do I Believe?

My father was a millionaire when I grew up — that is, when a million dollars was a lot of money. His definition of a man's success was: he makes a lot of money. I met and fell in love with a classical musician — who was never going to make a lot of money. We rocked along fine until we got *married*. Then I started to needle him about getting a "real job" where he could make lots of money. You see, I was operating from my father's Truth, having absorbed it as my own.

Fortunately, my husband was able to hold onto his truth about success: that it had little to do with money and a lot to do with happiness. I was forced to examine the Truth I was taught. I discovered I was living from a Truth that I didn't even believe. What I discovered was that *my* truth about success was much closer to my husband's truth than to my father's. My father was not a nice person. He made lots of money, but, because of his family of origin experiences, was not a nice person. Upon examining the Truth I was taught, I realized *my* truth about success had a lot to do with a person's character, about integrity, and about happiness. It had little to do with making lots of money. I also decided that another truth for me was that making a lot of money was fine. But that money never would be a higher value for me than personal integrity and happiness.

These are truths for *me*. I am not suggesting they be *your* truths. I am suggesting you figure out what your truths are. And to start living by them. You must go through the process of self-definition. First, become aware of what you were taught. Second, question it. Does it fit for you? Do you believe it? Do you believe it because you were taught it or do you really believe it? Third, adjust your truths. Redefine what you believe, what really fits for your soul. Ask yourself often, do I believe this or is it someone else's belief that I am living by? Something I was taught as Truth or something that's really true for me? If it doesn't feel quite right, chances are it's not really *your* belief system. When you truly self-define, it feels right. It fits.

Resistances

I've noticed two resistances to self-definition. The first is often a sense of guilt or a sense of betrayal of our parents. I've had many a person ask me about the Biblical commandment to honor thy father and mother. Also, people have described it to me as, "I feel like I'm being bad," or "I feel like I'm leaving my parents behind." Let me quote Kahlil Gibran from his book, *The Prophet*, which was written in 1923, when he is speaking of children:

> You may house their bodies but not their souls,
> For their souls dwell in the house of tomorrow, which you
>   cannot visit, not even in your dreams.
> You may strive to be like them, but seek not to make them like
>   you.
> For life goes not backwards nor tarries with yesterday.
> You are the bows from which your children as living arrows
>   are sent forth.

The order of the universe seems to say we are meant to leave our parents behind. We are meant to go beyond their level of awakening, their level of consciousness. What better way to honor them? We are meant to go forward. So, I say to you, it's *okay* to think differently than your parents, to go beyond where they have been. It's *okay* to self-define and discard some of the Truths your parents taught you. You can do it without guilt. Knowing, of course, our children will need to do the same.

The second resistance to self-definition I've noticed is usually less conscious. It's the longing to stay in that childlike place of being taken care of. The subconscious thought is: "If I self-define, who will take care of me? I'll have to take care of myself. No thanks! If I'm a "good son" and live by my parents' Truths then I don't have to take responsibility for my own happiness. After all, I'm doing the "right" thing so I will, therefore, still be taken care of."

I can only tell you that there is a level of denial — really dishonesty— in this strategy. You ARE responsible for your own life, number one. You are no longer a child. Number two, self-defining does not mean that you are giving up people loving you or caring for you. If anything, you will be more able to genuinely receive love and care if you have yourself clearly defined. You will not be selling your soul, so to speak, to be cared for. You can let go of the child ego that says take care of me because I can't, and adopt the adult ego that says even though I can care for myself, I value your caring for me and lovingly accept it.

Be True To Yourself

Life is such a personal journey. You are the only person with you 24-7. You're it. *This* person is who you need to have a clean relationship with. If you are at odds with yourself — if you are doing behaviors that do not fit with your own personal value system — you will feel a sense of bondage. It doesn't come from your partner — though it may feel that way. It comes from inside of YOU. It comes from not having a clear self-definition that you are living by. Once you begin to tell yourself the truth you can self-define. After that, get your behaviors congruent with that self-definition and you will experience personal freedom. Guaranteed.

Also, once you have developed a clear self-definition to live by (based on your own personal truths/beliefs), life becomes much simpler. Before you do or say anything, you simply have to check in with yourself and ask whether or not what you are about to say or do is congruent with WHO YOU ARE. If it's not, DON'T do it, DON'T say it. If it is, proceed. Say yes when you mean yes; no when you mean no. Vast amounts of struggle and confusion can literally disappear in your life overnight if you do this simple check-in.

We are all born with two things: our intellect and an opportunity to develop integrity. Now is the time for you to develop your integrity. And to live by it. To thine own self be true.

Being true to yourself also means DECIDING to respond to a situation rather than react to it. Take a pause before you say something and FIGURE IT OUT. Take a pause to make sure that what you are going to say fits with your value system, your beliefs (your truths), your personal integrity.

Years ago I was called to testify in a child molestation case where the child was my client, sent to me by Children's Protective Services. After extensive checks and balances from all different angles, I believed the child. In the courtroom, the accused was a young man, the mother's now ex-boyfriend. His attorney, assigned by the court, was pushy, aggressive, loud, and obnoxious. His job, of course, was to try to discredit my testimony. At one point, he came close to my face and practically screamed one of his questions at me. I sat there in silence, thinking. I wanted to make sure that everything I said was true and that it was consistent with my own integrity. I wanted to hold onto my personal power and not become reactionary to the attorney's intimidation tactics. Suddenly he asked me, dripping with sarcasm, if I had heard the question. I looked him square in the eye and politely, but firmly, responded, "Yes. I'm thinking."

It was at that moment I realized he cannot have my power — unless I give it to him. It was at that moment, too, I believe I established a new level of credibility with the jury. They saw I was not going to be reactionary. They saw that I had strength enough to hold onto myself in spite of the pressure to do otherwise, and that, I believe, added weight to my testimony. The young man was convicted. Later I found out that this wasn't the first time he had similar charges brought against him — by other ex-girlfriends' children.

The point is, there is power in being non-reactionary. If your wife or girlfriend or boss says something inflammatory to you, slow down. *Respond* rather than react. *Think* about what you want to say: is it true? Is it congruent with your self-definition? Is it in your best interest? People will test you on this. Especially a hurricaning partner. That's okay. You are capable, you are competent. Take your time, select your words carefully, and be true to yourself.

Chapter 10

Calming the Storm, Part I

In a way, everything in this chapter is something we've already talked about. Now's the time to take the tools you have learned — already have — and apply them to the hurricane. That is, you don't need any more tools than you have at this moment. You have everything you need. You're already there. You don't have to be bigger or better than you are right now, today. There are no extraordinary people, just ordinary people doing extraordinary things. All you need is practice — and gentleness with yourself when it doesn't go well the first 25 times.

Shamu

If you've ever visited one of the three Sea Worlds around the country you have undoubtedly seen Shamu, the whale. Shamu weighs up to 12,000 pounds and yet he is trained to jump some 20 feet into the air. You might wonder, how do they do that? Well, they use a method called operant conditioning that gradually "shapes" the whale's behavior. This method uses positive reinforcement to reward desired behavior. It is a very complex system, and so I speak of it here in simple terms.

In order to teach the whales to jump on cue, or "bow," the trainers begin with teaching each whale to touch the trainer's hand at the pool's waterline. For this the whale is rewarded. Gradually, and very incrementally, the trainer raises his or her hand, and again, the whale is rewarded for touching it. This process continues until the trainer can't reach any higher. At that point, a "target pole" is introduced about the length of a broomstick. This target pole has a ball on top of it which the whale gets rewarded for touching the same as the trainer's hand. It, too, is gradually, and very incrementally, raised. The process is slow, the process requires great patience and continuous positive reinforcement. Finally, a second, longer target pole is introduced and again, it is raised inch by inch to its full height. Soon, the whale is able to "bow" on cue, jumping — with its 12,000 pounds — completely out of the water. An amazing feat.

So, two points to take special note of. First, the whale is given ONLY positive reinforcement — and lots of it. And second, the training begins with touching the trainer's hand AT THE WATERLINE. That is, in the beginning, the whale is rewarded when there is *no jumping*. He or she is rewarded for many, many steps before *any* jumping is required.

So let it be with you. Take your goal of 'calming the storm' and break it down into *very small* steps. And then reward yourself greatly. Start at the waterline. Don't expect yourself to jump to 20' right out of the box and then beat yourself up because you couldn't do it. That's old behavior. You want to practice new behavior. Be gentle with yourself. Be honest with yourself. Start with low expectations, and then reward yourself greatly when you reach your target. And, as with Shamu, very GRADUALLY raise your pole. Each time give yourself positive reinforcement. Remember to say nice things to yourself. The goal is not to get discouraged. Calming a hurricane isn't easy — especially if you and your partner have an ingrained pattern. But you CAN do it. Begin at the waterline, be patient with yourself, go slowly, and reward yourself for *every* step along the way.

Also, read this whole chapter before you start. And then read it again. There are important tips here that you must integrate into your thinking to be successful at calming the storm and regaining your personal power.

Do Not Take Items Off the Table

First, do not take items off the table. Off-the-table items are topics that you avoid. They are the topics your wife most wants to talk about and the ones you least want to. They are the topics that most need to be resolved for your wife and the ones that seem the least resolvable to you. They are the topics she brings up over and over again. But here is the key: She doesn't keep bringing them up and talking about them incessantly to beat you up (though, of course, it may have that result). She keeps bringing them up and talking about them incessantly because she's stuck. She can't let go of the issue because it's not resolved, not fixed. She needs your help. She wants YOU to change a certain behavior so she can feel resolution.

I remember a client of mine whose wife raged at him, hurricaned relentlessly. He had weak ego strength and had difficulty setting boundaries. I told him to try to state clearly: I want to talk to you but I will not be verbally abused. I told him, if the behavior continued, to leave the house. At his next session he explained that he had done as I suggested and in leaving the house decided to go for a walk. He was utterly amazed as he exclaimed to me, "And do you know what she did? She put on her coat and came after me! She walked behind me and screamed some more — all the way down the street!" So, two things. Number one, next time take the car. And number two, note how very, very much she believes in YOUR ability to heal her pain. She keeps coming to you because she believes, deep in her soul, you can fix it. Heal her. Help her.

I believe that, too. You have tremendous healing power in the system. Tremendous. But you cannot heal the system if you routinely take things off the table and refuse to talk about them and listen to your wife's distress about them.

Remember Your Boundaries

That does not mean she is allowed to hurricane. That does not mean she is allowed to verbally batter you. That's where boundaries come in.

You cannot be hurricaned on or verbally battered if you have appropriate boundaries. Period. Let me state that again: you cannot be hurricaned on or verbally battered if you have appropriate boundaries. So, that means that your wife's hurricaning is a barometer for you. If SHE is hurricaning, YOU are off course. It is YOUR responsibility to have appropriate boundaries that say no to verbal battering. You are not a victim. You are not a child. Nobody else can do this for you. It is up to you to say no to bad treatment of you. You have to run the race. Nobody else can or will do it for you.

Appropriate boundaries include saying no when the answer is no. Saying yes when the answer is yes. Being true to yourself. Having absolutely ZERO tolerance for emotional and verbal battering. Removing yourself from the situation if you cannot stop the battering any other way.

I see removing yourself from the situation as a very primitive way to have a boundary, yet valid and necessary if you cannot stop the battering in any other peaceful way. It's a good thing. Primitive, but good. It's a beginning point. Starting at the waterline. I say this because I don't want you to think that leaving the situation every time is the goal. No, it is a first step. It is not where we are headed long term. It is what you may need to use now, before you can advance to a less primitive way of responding. Eventually you will be able to have boundaries without having to leave. This is a more advanced way of having a boundary. Start at the beginning, though. If you cannot hold onto your boundary in a peaceful way without leaving, then you MUST leave the situation rather than allowing yourself to be battered or sucked into playing ping pong.

The ultimate goal is to be able to stay with your partner in the process and actively participate in healing without being paralyzed by fear. However, that is advanced behavior. That is Shamu jumping out of the water 20'. You will, however, get there. Begin where you need to begin in order to have boundaries, but HAVE BOUNDARIES.

And don't take items off the table. Be willing to discuss the hard stuff. Have boundaries and a zero tolerance for verbal battering. Next, keep in mind that your partner is not your parent.

Claim Your Vote

She is not an authority figure in your life. You are not a child. She does not get to make all the rules. You are an adult and YOU get to make the rules for your life. You get to decide what works best for you: what feels right, what is congruent with your value system. That's what self-definition is about. And in the partnership, you get an equal vote on partnership rules. You are 50 percent of the system. Not 10 percent or 20 percent, a full half. And she is 50 percent of the system. Not 80 percent or 90 percent, but a mere half. You were unable to change the system with your parents. After all, children do not get equal votes with their parents. Now, however, you do. It's time to grow up and claim your full vote.

If my husband's out of town, my two boys will occasionally say to me, "We vote to go out to eat." If I want to go out, fine, we do. If I don't, I say, "Well, sorry, I vote against it." Then they shout foul! It's two votes to one! Then I say, "But ahhh, a mom's vote is worth five." They may still beg and plead and protest, but the point is: it's my car, it's my money, I decide if we go out or not. And if I say no, that's it. We're not going.

Thus it is in childhood. But *you are not a child any more*. As a child you did not get a full vote; as an adult, you do. Your wife is not your parent. She may remind you of your parent, but she is not your parent. Do not give your proxy vote to her. Do not put her in an authority figure role over you. You are not a second class citizen, so don't act like one. Claim your vote.

Counter-Instinctual

In order to do this, you have to get okay with confrontation and okay with fear. Remember, based on what happened to you in your childhood, you may have an automatic response to anger or confrontation. You may automatically — without thought — revert back to that scared place where you instinctively fight or flight to survive. DO NOT give into this instinct. Yes, I am asking you to be counter-instinctual. I am asking you to become aware of that feeling of life or death/fight or flight survival response. Then I am asking you to intervene with yourself. You will need to activate a voice of reason in your head. Your emotional self will want to run for your life. It's time for your rational self to slow things down and tell yourself the truth. Your life is not being threatened. You are safe. You are an adult and you can keep yourself safe. You do not have to fight or run away. Fear is only a feeling. This is not a life or death survival situation. It's only your wife being in pain about something. She wants you to heal her and she's telling you in the best way she knows how. It's a primitive way: yelling and screaming and being relentless, but an effort on her part nonetheless. You need to have a boundary here. You are not going to die. Her being in distress is not life threatening. Help her. Don't run away. Don't go inside yourself. Don't lash out. You are safe. You do not need to defend yourself.

In the movie, *The Sixth Sense*, the main character was a young boy who saw dead people. He was terrified of them. He ran from them, withdrew, hid in terror. His therapist helped him learn not to run and to face his fears. He helped him learn to actually turn around, go back to the dead person, and ask them what they wanted. This was not easy for the boy to do. Every fiber in his body said RUN! He had to learn, so beautifully portrayed in the movie, not to run. He had to learn to respond in a counter-instinctual way and do the *exact opposite* of what came automatically, instinctually. He learned to change his inner self-talk and to go back and ask the dead people what they wanted. He also learned not to be afraid and was able to completely regain his personal power and his life.

So will you. As you say this self-talk over and over again in the moment, your body chemistry will relax. Your body will stop pumping in adrenalin that gives you inaccurate information about the situation. You must learn to calm your body by using this self-talk so you can have the presence of mind to have a boundary, and to remain present for the healing process. This is counter-instinctual, I realize. It is possible, however — and necessary — to shut down that instinct and to respond from a rational part of your brain.

It is okay, too, to talk about this in advance with your wife. Tell her you need her to talk to you in a different way when she is upset. Tell her you need her to talk quietly, in a soft voice. Tell her you need her not to scream at you because then you tend to get instinctual on her, fight or flight, and lose your ability to hear her. Explain the system to her. Have her read this book. Take action before you need to. That is, get your tools out before there is a hurricane.

Be Proactive

In other words, be proactive. Being proactive at its best means dealing with a problem at point A rather than waiting until it's developed to point B or C or even D or E. It does NOT mean dealing with the problem at point M or N. It means dealing with it immediately. It means nipping the hurricane in the bud as soon as the winds start blowing. This is probably THE most important element in calming the storm. Calm it when it's little. *Be proactive.* Don't wait until it's full blown. Talk about a problem the moment you become aware of it. *Bring it up.* Say, "I want to talk about what's bothering you," and then, "What do you need from me?" Be proactive. Take charge. Apologize if there's something you need to apologize for. Do not wait until your wife's energy is at overwhelmingly large proportions.

Ruptures

In a healthy relationship, we are "connected" to our partner. There is a flow of energy between husband and wife. The goal is to keep that connection intact. It is similar to an electrical current. If there is a break in the circuit between the electrical source and the electrical outlet, of course the outlet won't work. This is similar in intimate relationships. If there's a rupture in the energy flow between husband and wife, the relationship won't work. The winds of the storm will begin to blow.

The ideal is to stay emotionally connected to our partner *always*. Not to be enmeshed. Not to disappear. Not to blend the electrical source and the electrical outlet together, but to learn how to keep the electricity flowing between the two solid, separate entities. That is, to prevent a rupture in connection from happening.

The reality, however, is that ruptures WILL happen. Because you're not perfect, because your partner's not perfect, ruptures will happen. Therefore, the best we can hope for is to get really good at recognizing when a rupture has occurred, and to develop the ability to immediately respond to it. When a rupture happens, there's a wound that needs immediate attention. If the wound is attended to immediately, then there isn't going to be anything big or dramatic coming out of it. Think of a rupture in connection as equal to a water pipe bursting in your house. Would you stand there and watch it pump more and more water into your home before taking action? Would you sit down and drink your morning coffee before turning off the water supply to your home? What if it were a fire? Would you wait an hour or two before doing anything? A day? A week? A month? What if your child ran in screaming with his arm ripped open and bleeding profusely from a dog bite? Would you say to yourself, "Well, I'll deal with that later"?

My point is, though it may not be as visible as the above examples, a rupture in the connection of your relationship is an emergency that needs your full and IMMEDIATE attention. That is, if you treat a rupture in connection as an emergency, you will prevent disaster. On the other hand, if you are oblivious to the rupture or choose to ignore it, it is as though you are throwing a burning match into a can of gasoline. I cannot emphasize this enough. DO NOT let the rupture go unattended. It will not magically heal on its own. You must attend to it.

Codependency

Now you may be saying to yourself, aren't you advocating codependency? No, I'm not. I hate codependency. Codependency to me is two half people together in a relationship instead of two whole people. I think of a healthy relationship as having three complete parts: a whole "I", a whole "you," and a whole "us." Codependency is more like just an "us." It's a relationship that sucks the life out of people. What I'm advocating is that both people have their own personal power and ability to be fully connected to their own life force. When each individual can stand whole alone, he/she can then be fully present to a partner. Then the relationship becomes an energizer. Then the emotional, physical, intellectual, and spiritual parts of each person can thrive.

Codependency is not about that. Codependency is having an over-reaction to things outside of the self (like you can tell me what your partner's thinking, how she'll react, what makes her angry, what's acceptable to her and what isn't, what she feels and values, etc.) and an under-reaction to things inside of the self (you cannot tell me those things about yourself). The goal here is self-definition, not codependency. You must know yourself — and know yourself well — to calm the storm and realign your system.

That is, you must HAVE a self to be proactive. This book is about having a self — all of you, including the emotional part that got squelched somewhere in your history. Codependency prevents that.

Speaking With Love In Your Voice

One last tool: As obnoxious as it may sound, you must practice speaking sweetly. This is especially important if your coping mechanism has been "fight." Consider Newton Hightower's story. Newton is an excellent therapist in Houston who works with men who have rage problems. In his own journey Newton tells of losing two marriages because of his rage. Early in his third marriage, much to his chagrin, he raged again. His wife responded by saying, "If you ever do that to me again, I will divorce you," to which Newton sadly acknowledged, "I know."

That day Newton decided to get sober. He kept a calendar and checked it off day after day: no rage. Finally, after a year he said to his wife, "It's been a whole year and I haven't raged once." She stunned him by saying, "You're no better than you ever were. You speak to me in that condescending, mean tone everyday." You see, he was still angry, he was still harsh, he was still brutal with his words.

He had to learn to say things nicely, lovingly, sweetly. He had to learn to speak with tenderness. And he did. And so can you. Today Newton teaches 280 pound raging Vietnam Vets to get sober from their rage, and to speak sweetly. It's an invaluable tool.

Review

So let's review calming the storm and the tools we've talked about so far.

- Be gentle with yourself and patient with yourself.
- Practice everyday, and gradually raise your bar.
- Do not take items off the table.
- Remember that your wife is wounded and is asking for healing (in a primitive, not very effective way).
- Set boundaries — do NOT allow yourself to be raged at.

- Do not give your vote away — hold onto yourself. Remember your wife is not your parent.
- Remind yourself that you are safe and not a child.
- Be counter-instinctual (calm your fight or flight natural reaction) since talking with your partner is not life threatening.
- Be proactive: bring things up that need to be resolved.
- Attend to a rupture in connection immediately.
- Practice speaking with love in your voice.

Chapter 11

Calming the Storm, Part II

Silence is not golden. Silence is a form of relationship suicide. Silence DOES NOT make a rupture with your partner better. It makes it worse. Period. You have to talk. I know that talking may not come naturally to you. This is especially true if you were silenced as a child and now are in the pattern of being silenced by your partner. Nonetheless, it is essential that you exercise your voice.

Many men say to me, "I don't talk because I don't know what to say." Well, now's the time to know. You are capable of figuring it out. You are not a child anymore. You can think, you can guess, you can figure it out. Think it through and say something. Some men I work with talk inside their heads instead of out of their mouths. They THINK they are saying *out loud* what they are saying *in their heads*. If your partner keeps expressing frustration with you because you are not talking, you are NOT saying the things in your head out loud. You must practice saying the things out of your mouth and checking with your partner to see if she heard you. Use your words. Otherwise you are simply encouraging a bad relationship and inviting the storm into your life.

The goal is to have an energized, loving, life-supporting, fun marriage. You deserve that. But it won't happen if you can't talk. A rule of thumb is: talk about it more than you want to. One of my client's told me, "If I'm comfortable, I know I'm off track." And he's right, because *new* behavior is *un*comfortable — at first. For ANYONE. And talking about tough issues longer than is comfortable for you is new behavior. It won't feel good — at first. It won't feel good for three months. Keep talking. Eventually it will become second nature.

Talking Tips

Here are just a couple of simple talking tips. When you are talking with your partner it should feel somewhat like an easy volley of tennis. Not a tennis match where you are competing and trying to win, but an easy volley back and forth over the net. There should be almost a rhythm. You talk. She talks. You talk. She talks. There needs to be a flow to the conversation: a giving, a taking, a giving, a taking, etc. Think of it as ice skates on smooth ice — left then right then left then right. This means, don't make the pauses too long. Unless your wife also has long pauses, the rhythm of the conversation gets off. Try to respond right away to what your partner just said. Yes, you can always take some time and think about what she said — tell her you're thinking — and try to keep the easy volley going.

This is not the same as playing ping-pong where you shoot one cutting remark after another back and forth between the two of you. No, this is a cooperative interacting that supports the relationship instead of ripping it down.

Another talking tip is: don't be predictable. Don't do and say all the things you have done and said 1000 times before. How boring. Try saying something new. When your wife says something insulting to you, instead of your predictable behavior which might be withdrawing into silence or walking away or reacting with an insult back, do something different. Say something different. Say, "Honey, that's so insulting to me. I don't want to be insulted anymore. I don't want a marriage full of insults. I want you to know I love you and I want to know you love me even when we're angry with each other. I want things to be different between us — not the same. Don't you?" Shake it up a bit.

Healing Words

Another talking tip is: get comfortable saying you're sorry. These words, along with behavioral change, are THE words that heal. How damaged your relationship is will determine how long and how often you will have to say them. If you've had an affair or multiple affairs the healing time is about 5 years. You'll have to say, "I'm sorry," almost daily for the first month or two, maybe three. I have men that say, "No way!" and I say, "Way." "I'm sorry" does not diminish you. "I'm sorry" gives you power to heal.

I'm not talking about groveling. No. Never grovel. You are better than that. I am talking about learning how to acknowledge pain you have created and to apologize for it. This is an adult behavior — as compared to child behavior of minimizing or avoiding. Learning how to say, "Yes, I did that. I was wrong. I wish I had never done that. I'm sorry," and then saying it again. "I'm sorry I hurt you. I wish I had never hurt you. I wish I could go back in time and do it differently," and then saying it again. "I'm sorry. I want you to know I'm not doing that behavior anymore. I am committed to never doing that behavior again. I'm sorry I ever did that behavior knowing how much pain it has caused. I wish I could do it over again." And then saying it again.

Remember you are healing your partner. Your words are like salve to a wound. She may resist them. She may minimize them. She may discard them completely and throw them back in your face. That just tells you how deep her wounds are. Keep saying them. Day after day, "I'm sorry." "I'm sorry for the past. I hope we can get beyond that. I'm not that person anymore. I'm doing things differently now. I need you to get that at a deep level, and I know it will take time. I wish I had never hurt you and we didn't have this mess to clean up."

Now, it's a given that these words need to be sincere. Are you sorry? Are you sorry for the pain you've caused? Now, with hindsight, do you wish you'd made different choices and been a more responsible or more committed partner? Are you sorry you didn't have the awareness then that you have now? Are you actually making behavioral changes to clean up the wreckage of the past and not create new wreckage? Do you really get it and are you really sorry?

Walk the Walk

My husband and I used to have a struggle every year about doing the taxes. We both hated to do them, and so, procrastinated and procrastinated even starting them. Yet, inevitably, *I* would be the one that took responsibility and began the process. Then it would be like pulling teeth. Since my husband and I are both self-employed, we both needed to bring our records to the table. I would do my part. He would not. Then for two months — sometimes more — I would nag and bitch and moan about it trying to get him to get his numbers in order. Sometimes I'd yell. Sometimes I'd cry. But always I'd bring it up, and bring it up, and bring it up.

Then one year I decided this was a miserable experience. (Duh. I'm not sure why it takes us doing things miserably for a while before we realize we need to change things, but we do. It seems to be part of the human condition.) So one day I got it — it clicked — and I decided I didn't want to do it like we had been doing it anymore. I pointed out our pattern to my husband. He agreed it was miserable. He agreed he was the one who was the biggest "stuck" in the system. He really looked at his resistance. He apologized. He realized he was causing pain and could do it differently. He resolved to change his behavior.

And didn't.

He said he would. He apologized. He said he was committed to doing it differently. He apologized some more. I believed him. But the behavior didn't change, so it didn't count. I finally said to him, "You're saying the right words, but your behavior is the same. Is this just about talking the talk or are you going to walk the walk?" Talking the talk is the easy part. It's not enough.

But, I also want you to know that walking the walk is not enough, either. You also need words. I hear from men, "Well, she won't believe words. I'll just show her with my behavior." Wrong. You also need words. Now, I'll admit, if you can only do one thing — either talking the talk or walking the walk — walking the walk is the one to choose. But I also know, that the fastest healing comes when you do both.

She needs to hear words of reassurance and words of ownership. Say the words. Apologize. And then apologize again. Verbal acknowledgment of the wounding you have caused, taking ownership of your hurtful behavior OUT LOUD to your partner, is healing. Is necessary. Of course the words have to be sincere, and of course the behavioral change has to be measurable, but remember, one without the other is not enough. Say the words. Apologize. Acknowledge your screw up. This is so validating to your partner. It says, "You are not crazy. You're right. That happened." This will ease the pain tremendously for her. This will be healing if accompanied by different behavior on your part.

My husband had to get to a different level of self-honesty about how he was doing the taxes. He was creating a lot of frustration in our marriage by saying one thing and doing another. He realized he wasn't in personal integrity. He either had to stop saying he would do it differently or do it differently. He decided to do it differently since dragging it out was a miserable experience for him, too. First of all, it felt like a monkey he had to carry around on his back for months and he was tired of toting around that monkey. Secondly, it made me really unhappy and he gets lots more positives from me when I'm happy. He changed his accounting system at work and he simplified his tax approach. He took charge of the situation, got proactive, got out of the victim role, and changed it.

Remember, You are not a victim when you are working to calm the storm. Take responsibility for your part. Are you doing something to encourage the storm? Take ownership of it. Talk about it, apologize, and then CHANGE it.

Clean Your Side of the Street

I can hear lots of people in the background crying, "Foul! Foul!" What about your wife's part? What about the things SHE does that are outrageous and unhealthy and create wreckage? Surely I'm not saying that a relationship's not working is all the MAN'S fault? No, I'm not. I'm saying YOUR half of the relationship not working is 100%, totally, completely, your "fault." A better word for me is, your "responsibility." We are only looking at your side of the equation in this side of the book. The other side of this book is written for women to look at their side of the equation. You do not have to fix the whole equation. You do have to fix your part of it. This is done by accepting complete, 100 percent responsibility for everything you are thinking, feeling, doing, or not doing. It is letting go of blaming ANYone for ANYthing. It is growing up and being an adult. It is taking the "blame" off your wife and honestly looking at what needs to change in YOUR behavior to make your marriage wonderful. Let her worry about cleaning up her own stuff. You concentrate on cleaning up yours. Get in integrity with yourself.

Safety

Healthy, wonderful, fun relationships are built on safety. Are you making things safe — emotionally safe — for your partner? You can heal your relationship by doing so. How does one provide emotional safety? Tell the truth. Talk. Face the hard stuff. Apologize. Have boundaries. Be proactive. All of these behaviors that we have talked about provide emotional safety. All of these behaviors are healing.

You are capable of being a positive force on this earth. Healing your marriage – fixing what is broken by providing emotional safety – will heal generations. Not only will you and your wife be happier, your kids will be happier which will make their kids happier, etc. Do not underestimate your healing power. It is mammoth.

Responding

Remember, too, calming the storm means learning to respond rather than react. **Responding means choosing**. Responding means figuring out your choices and picking one *on purpose*. It means slowing things down long enough to *think*.

Here are two specific choices that will help you get out of reactive behavior:

1. *Make your wife's behavior about her and not you.* She is wounded and trying to tell you about it. She needs something from you to help her heal. Try to figure out what it is.

2. *Make it small.* In AA there's a saying, "Don't sweat the small stuff and remember it's all small stuff." See the forest – don't get stuck on a tree. The forest is: you want a better relationship. A tree is only that: a tree. Small.

All this is to say, when you consciously examine your choices and consciously pick one that you feel is congruent with your goals and personal integrity, then you are responding and not reacting. Proactive, on purpose, slowed down thinking will aid in calming any storm that may blow your way. One last thing about choosing/responding. If you make a conscious choice (well thought out and picked on purpose) based on the information you have at the time, it's a good choice. Period. There are no bad conscious choices. If, down the line, you get further information that says that your first choice is not going to be effective, then you just make another choice. It doesn't make your first decision bad or wrong. If you had the information *then* that you have *now*, you would have made a different choice originally. But you didn't have that information then. So, based on what you knew and considered at the time, you made a good choice. Period.

Win/Win

Last but not least in calming the storm, focus on creating win/win. The goal is for you to win and for your partner to win. The goal is NOT for your partner to win and for you to lose.

One of my clients had parents who used to trade off days being dead. They would actually say out loud — and in front of the children — "It's your day to be dead." What that meant was: shut up, I'm in charge today, everything goes as I choose, you don't count. How bizarre is that? And yet that's what we do to each other if we set up win/lose situations. Either I get to be dead today or you do. That's not okay. In your marriage, each person deserves to be fully alive — everyday. This can only happen if we let go of the concept that "marriage is a compromise."

No Compromising

How many times have you heard: in marriage you just have to compromise? I'm here to tell you that I, for one, don't believe that. I don't believe that because I've seen over and over again that it doesn't work. This is because people define the word "compromise" as, "It's your day to be dead." Compromise doesn't work when it means we take turns losing. I lose, you win, or, Yeah! I win, you lose. It's your day to compromise. I was dead last time, so it's your turn this time.

To many people, compromise also seems to mean giving in. Saying, "Yes," when they want to say, "No." Giving up. Saying, "Whatever!" to keep the peace. "Compromise" often is about giving your power away. Feeling powerless. Feeling like you have no choice. I hear, "It's a big deal to her so okay. Fine. We'll do it that way." But when I press deeper, it's really not fine. Not fine at all. The husband is saying yes when it's really not yes at all. Then he blurts out, "Well, isn't that how I'm supposed to do it? After all, marriage is a compromise, right?" And I say, "Wrong."

I take a counter view that says marriage is not a compromise. In fact, I believe, even in marriage — especially in marriage — one should *never* compromise. That is: one should *never compromise oneself.* In a nutshell, that's why I don't think compromise in marriage works: because it so often gets interpreted as compromising oneself.

In general, I am not very black and white in my thinking. I don't live life in an all or nothing way. But on this point, I do. Try NEVER to compromise yourself, and remember you ALWAYS have choice. This concept needs to be imbedded in you as deeply as we NEVER have sex with our children. It is NEVER okay. It's the same with compromising oneself. If you are saying yes when the answer is no, giving in in the name of compromise, please stop. It doesn't work. It only violates your soul. It leads to feelings of anger and resentment. It leads to feelings of entrapment and powerlessness. It leads to underground acting out.

So how on earth are two people supposed to live together in harmony since at one thousand junctures they'll have different opinions and desires? The answer is to learn yourself and to learn how to never compromise that self. The answer is to learn how to only say yes when the answer is yes. The answer is to learn to create win/win situations everyday in every interaction you have.

Hierarchy of Values

You may be asking, how do I do that? Of course with boundaries, of course with self-knowledge, of course with non-victim, but also, you will need to get conscious of the hierarchy of values and goals that you operate under. We all have this hierarchy. Some things are more important to us than others. Oxygen is more important to us than sex, for example. Emotionally, things are more and less important to us, too. Start defining that for yourself. This will allow you to always be true to yourself and yet be able to live in harmony with other people. This will allow you to come from a position of choice, and not a position of compromise.

Let me explain. My husband and I recently bought a pop-up

camper. Now, I enjoy camping, but if we went once a year that would be enough for me. My two boys, however, love camping and were dying for a pop-up. My husband said he thought it was a good idea and voted for it. I was the holdout. I had to figure out could I say yes to this wholeheartedly? Could I honestly, without compromising myself, say yes to something that at first glance was a definite, "No way!" I had to look deeper. I had to go into my hierarchy of goals and values.

On vacations, I value hotels. I like to be pampered, I like to eat out every meal, I like someone to make the beds and clean the bathroom while I'm out having fun. But I also value family. And good parenting. In my good parenting value is my goal of giving the kids fun memories, adventures, family togetherness. I began to see that having a pop-up camper may allow us to have more of those moments. It's cheaper than staying in hotels and eating out every meal. I started thinking that it would allow the kids to bring along friends more often if we took little mini-trips. Also, our family likes to play games together. Suddenly I had a flash of our sitting around the table in that little camper engaged in a great game of *Scattegories* or playing cards. I was getting closer to being able to say yes without compromise. Without having to give in and feel like I lost something.

I talked to my husband about it and asked if we bought the camper was he thinking we wouldn't be taking any more vacations in hotels? No, he wasn't thinking that. I looked at would we have to give those up financially? We talked about taking one hotel trip a year — instead of our normal two — and then taking several mini-vacations in the camper. I thought to myself, "Well, that would actually be nice. That could work for me." Now I was ready to say yes to the camper. I had no resentment. I felt complete choice. We had worked to come up with a win/win situation that both my husband and I could wholeheartedly say yes to.

In your relationship, you must do the same. Do not say fine to stuff that's not fine. Look at your hierarchy of goals and values. Dig deeper. If a higher value will allow you to say yes to something that initially looked like a no, then you can say yes cleanly. Just make sure you have taken a deeper look at any resistance to an idea you might have had and decide — make a choice — as to whether or not you are wholeheartedly able to let go of that resistance. You will only be able to let go of it if you have a higher value that you want to be true to. But, DO NOT say yes to something when the answer is no.

I've had men — and women — who have said yes to giving up friendships, sports activities, going fishing on Saturday mornings, and too often their dreams in the name of compromise. It's time to stop doing that. If after examining your hierarchy of goals and values you CHOOSE to give something up — that's different. That's okay. Like, because I'm married I choose not to date other people and I choose not to keep up relationships with past boyfriends. Why? Not because they aren't wonderful people. Not because there aren't lots of fantastic guys around that are interesting. But because my higher value is that I want my husband to feel safe, to feel valued, to feel loved. Those other people are not more important to me than he is. I also know that if he feels safe and valued and loved, *I'm* going to get more out of the relationship.

No Room For Blame

A twist to this theme is the person who says no to something because his wife wants him to without really even examining if his answer is yes or no. Just going along because her answer is no and then resenting her. For example, I had a client who hated his job and fantasized about opening a bed and breakfast. When asked why he didn't pursue that dream, he blamed his wife. "Oh, she won't go along with it. She likes the money too much. We have arguments about it all the time." I smelled a victim stance. "I'm a victim here. I can't do what I want because of my wife. My wife won't let me." I told him to take his wife out of the picture and talk to me about his dream of running a bed and breakfast. What attracted him to that idea? At first he couldn't tell me, but then he was able to come up with the word "escape." Turns out that in his hierarchy of goals and values he valued autonomy highly. Turns out, too, that he was in a job where he didn't have much sense of power or autonomy.

On further examination he realized that he wouldn't really even like running a bed and breakfast. He didn't like other people in his house, he certainly wouldn't want to wait on them, he wouldn't like the low income, and he realized it wouldn't give him the sense of power and autonomy he wanted anyway. He was able to let go of his anger and resentment toward his wife because he "wasn't allowed to have his dream." He decided instead to consciously decide — to choose — to let go of his "dream" and to pursue what he really wanted: a different job where he could be his own boss, make lots of money, and get the autonomy and sense of personal power he so longed for.

He left his engineering job of 22 years and opened a consulting firm. He loves it. He works less and makes more money. And it came from HIS saying no to holding onto his "dream". Before, he blamed his wife's saying no to his dream and his willingness to agree — resentfully — to her restriction. He was agreeing to a win/lose situation to keep his wife happy. Only after he took ownership of HIS no to really wanting the "dream" could he get unstuck, move on, and create a win/win solution.

True To Yourself

The goal is win/win. Always. You win, I win. You get to be alive, I get to be alive. The solution works for you, and it works for me. Anything less than that — especially in the name of compromise — only leads to relationships that don't work. Do not compromise yourself. Look for ways that you might be able to say yes without resentment. Look at your hierarchy of goals and values. If, after examining them, you find you have a higher value than the current one you have resistance to, then you can say yes cleanly. If you don't have a higher value that you can commit to in order to say yes, then the answer is no. Period.

I had a client one time whose boss wanted him to quote one price on a job and bill another. He was told if he didn't do it he would be fired. Now, he had a wife and two children and was the sole financial supporter of the family. He also didn't have a college degree and had managed to work his way up in the company to a pretty good paying job with some authority. He liked his job. He looked at his values and goals hierarchy. He valued taking care of his family. He valued being happy in a job. But he also valued being a good role model to his kids. He also valued personal integrity. He said, "How can I teach them to live in personal integrity when I'm willing to sell mine out for money?" He decided that even though it would be risky financially to say no to his boss, that it was more risky to *himself* to say yes. He said no, his boss found ways to fire him, he got fired. Ultimately, though, he was glad he had stuck to his no. He says in retrospect, "Yeah, that was a scary time, but I'm glad I did it. I can look myself in the eye, I can sleep soundly at night. And, hey, I'm not working for a jerk anymore." If the answer's no, the answer's no. If a higher level on your hierarchy of values can't get you to a yes, the answer's no.

Retraction

I don't want to suggest that you will ALWAYS get it right. Perfection is not the goal here. Sometimes you may — even without thinking — say yes to something and then kick yourself for it later. At that point you have two choices. Number one, you can choose to get okay with having said yes, or number two, you can retract your yes and say no.

When the birth of my second child was imminent, I was talking to my mother on the phone. We were planning for her to come to help out for a couple of weeks when the baby came. I told her that as soon as I went into labor I would call her and she could catch the first plane here. Then the thought occurred to me that, if I had a long labor, she might even make it to the hospital before he was born. I blurted this out and then added, "Would you like to be in the room when he's born?" Oh, she was thrilled! "YES!" she said. She would love that. Then she went on and on and on about how special that would be, how wonderful, how she couldn't believe I would even ask her, etc. I hung up the phone and thought to myself, "WHAT was I thinking? Do I want my MOTHER at the birth of my child?" My gut was screaming, NO! Now, I love my mother dearly, but I started thinking how very sacred and personal a child birthing experience is. I wanted to share this with my HUSBAND — not my MOTHER! I asked my husband what it would be like for him if my mother were there, and his response was something like, "Are you crazy?! I don't want your MOTHER there!" He had confirmed exactly what I had been feeling.

So, even though it was hard, I called my mother back and *uninvited* her to the childbirth. I can tell you she was very disappointed, but I can also tell you the moon didn't fall out of the sky. Nothing horrible, nothing horrific happened because I went back and retracted my yes.

Learn how to say, "You know, I agreed to that, but I've thought it over, and that just won't work for me. I'm sorry. I've really got to say no to that." Practice these words. Nothing horrible, nothing horrific will happen. If your partner starts to hurricane, remember your boundaries. You are not a victim. If you need to go back and retract a yes, go back and retract it.

Credibility

Now, I don't suggest you do this on a regular basis. If you do, you will lose your credibility. You will come to be seen as someone who can't be counted on. But, I am suggesting it's okay to do this on occasion. The ideal, of course, is to really think through your answer before you open your mouth. The ideal is that you only say yes when the answer is yes. However, because of your humanness, you — like everyone else — will find you've said yes to something when the answer is actually no. That's when it's okay to retract.

It's also okay, on occasion, to bite the bullet and choose to keep your original "yes" for the sake of practicing keeping your word. For example, if you tell your wife you'll mow the lawn after work, and then when you get home from work, you are exhausted and do not in

ANY way feel like mowing the lawn, you might at that point *decide* to bite the bullet. Do it anyway. Admit to yourself, "No, I don't want to do the yard but I'm going to because I said I would. I've got to get better at keeping my word — I back out too often." And you go and mow the yard. In this case, it's a contract you've made with yourself. Get it off your wife. It's not about mowing the lawn to keep her happy or keep her off your back. It's about mowing the lawn to keep *you* happy. To keep your contract with yourself about improving your ability to keep your word. It's about helping you feel good about you.

The Starfish

Keep in mind, perfection is not the name of the game. Do the best you can and keep practicing. I'm reminded of a story my minister told one time. It's the starfish story. A child was walking the shore early in the morning after the tide had gone out. The beach was scattered with hundreds of starfish. The little boy was picking them up and throwing them back into the ocean. A stranger came along amazed by this sight and asked the child what he was doing. The boy explained that if a starfish was not put back into the ocean that it would die. Then the stranger exclaimed, "But surely you can't possibly believe that your throwing a few starfish back into the ocean even matters. Surely you must know there are hundreds — maybe thousands — of starfish on probably hundreds of beaches that die every day."

To that the child picked up a starfish and sent it flying back into the ocean. He looked up at the stranger and said, "It mattered to that one."

You see, EVERY time you use new, healthier behavior where you are more honest, more true to yourself, more connected to your personal integrity, it counts. *Every* time.

Chapter 12

The Journey Continues

I'd like to tell you that once you have learned to calm the storm, hold onto your personal power, have boundaries, feel your feelings, be honest with yourself, and live in personal integrity, that you have *arrived*. But, that's not true. There is not an arrival *point*. It is an ongoing journey. Yes, how cliche. But I tell you it's a cliche because it is true. You must remain — for the rest of your life — ever vigilant. Ever vigilant in choosing integrity.

Now, I will tell you it does get better. It does get easier. It does become second nature where you don't have to do a lot of thinking about it. It does become integrated into who you are, and it feels good. But you still have to remain what I call "conscious." You still have to remain aware of your choices — and that you HAVE choices — and that you must, one time after the next, choose the most self-honest one.

It's rather like exercising. If you are out of shape — even dreadfully, pathetically out of shape — you can change that. You can slowly but surely, one step in front of the next, begin a walking program. Maybe you'll start by walking slowly 5 minutes a day. Gradually you add more time to your program and then add speed. Eventually, *if you remain true to your program*, you WILL get in shape. But what happens when you are in great shape, physical activity is easy for you and feels fun, and you decide to take a few years off to sit on the couch and watch TV? Now, you won't lose all the health benefits you gained from the years of being in shape, or the emotional benefits, for that matter, but you will lose being in shape, obviously. The point is, being "in shape" isn't an arrival point that once you reach you will forever have. It's not like climbing Mt. Everest where once you've done that you will have forever done that. No, with being in shape, if you never do another physical activity in your life, you can count on flab setting in.

Likewise with your emotional self. Once you get in touch with your feelings and experience living in personal integrity with your whole self, you can never completely lose that, but you must exercise your new tools to stay in shape. This concept is captured so well in the Tenth Step of the Twelve Step Programs. Step 10: "Continue to take personal inventory and when we are wrong, promptly admit it." Continue to take personal inventory. That's the part I'm talking about. Keep checking in with yourself. Keep checking to see if you are walking in personal integrity. Self-correct where you need to.

I want to tell you the story of Johnny Ray Youngblood, with his permission, of course. Johnny Ray is the minister of a large church in New York City. But it wasn't always that way. When he began his ministry in 1974 at Saint Paul Community Baptist Church, the congregation was a mere 84 people. Years earlier, this church boasted a membership of over five hundred. What happened? By the time Johnny Ray got there in 1974, the church was, literally, falling apart. The roof had leaks, there were holes in the walls, the paint was cracked and peeled off, the plumbing was broken, and people were not coming to church. The few who did come weren't able to pledge any money — they were poor. Many people were disillusioned and turned their backs on the church. The church was dying.

Then in steps Johnny Ray Youngblood. Young, charismatic, somewhat naive, but tenacious, he decided to systematically turn that church around. First, he would make one visual improvement to the church each week. One week it was a beautiful drawing of the church posted on the bulletin board. The next brought a new finish to a door. Then the holes in the walls got patched, the plumbing fixed, tile added, etc. His next plan of attack was his personal commitment to himself to get to know every single member of that congregation. He held meetings, he held pot lucks, he held picnics.

Now Johnny Ray has a tremendous memory. That was a good thing in 1974. It allowed him to look out from the pulpit on Sunday mornings and call out people's names as he looked at them. People began to feel noticed, valued, important. People began to feel part of something greater than themselves. They began to volunteer at the church, pledge money, serve on committees. They began to dream along with Johnny Ray. Not surprisingly, the church started to grow. It grew into a formidable force in the neighborhood. They cleaned up the streets, got rid of the crack houses, built a school, started a drug rehab program. In a few short years, that Johnny Ray Youngblood's church grew into a church of thousands.

Yet still, he questioned himself.

Was the church doing enough? Was the church getting too big? Were there deep level changes happening or did they just look good? Was church becoming too much of a "production"? Was it — was he — becoming stale? Was he loosing touch?

And then one day, in 1990, Johnny Ray had his answer. He walked into a neighborhood store and the clerk asked him if he had a brother who was a minister. He said no, and the conversation continued until she asked, "You know Johnny Youngblood?"

"Yeah, I know him. I *am* him."

So embarrassed, the clerk blurted out, "Oh, my God. My pastor," to which Johnny Ray, stunned but keeping his composure, smiled and asked, "And who, are you?"

This short, seemingly insignificant interaction rocked Johnny Ray to his core. He was gravely distressed. At that moment he remembered his commitment to himself to know his congregants. He felt sick. He had never seen this woman before. And he realized he hadn't seen lots of people who sat in his pews. He had been so busy growing and building.

Johnny Ray hired an outsider as a consultant to tell him and his church staff what decay needed to be cleared away. What fat needed to be trimmed. What denial needed to be confronted.

Ever vigilant. Johnny Ray recommitted himself to himself. He recommitted to being more authentic. He recommitted himself to knowing his people. He reconnected to himself — again. He reconnected to his church — again.

And we all have to do it again. And again. And again. Get real with ourselves. Get honest with ourselves. There is no arrival *point*. You've got to *keep* being clean with yourself and with your partner. You've got to decide daily — at each crossroad — on personal integrity. Over, and over, and over again.

The hope is in the fact that every time you choose it, it counts. Every time you choose honesty over fear, it counts. Every time you choose response over reaction, it counts. Every time you CHOOSE — versus being whisked along without thought — it counts.

You can do it. You are bright. You are capable. You are competent. And you are in the process of doing it right now. Keep going. As one of your coaches, I support you in your efforts and say to you: Go the distance.

GO THE DISTANCE.

I also say to you: read the other side of this book. It will help you get to the finish line quicker.

Recommended Reading

Adult Children of Alcoholics by Janet Geringer Woititz

Anger Busting 101 by Newton Hightower

Boundaries by Henry Cloud and John Townsend

Driven To Distraction by Edward Hallowell and John Ratey

The Emotional Incest Syndrome by Pat Love

Feel the Fear and Do It Anyway by Susan Jeffers

Getting the Love You Want by Harville Hendrix

The Life You've Always Wanted by John Ortberg

Man's Search for Meaning by Viktor E. Frankl

The Prophet by Kahlil Gibran

Seven Habits of Highly Effective Families by Stephen R. Covey

Too Good to Leave, Too Bad to Stay by Mira Kirshenbaum

Upon This Rock: Miracles of a Black Church by Samuel G. Freedman

What to Say When You Talk to Yourself by Shad Helmstetter

Who Moved My Cheese? by Spencer Johnson

Index

Y

FLIP BOOK OVER
to read the women's side of the book

FLIP BOOK OVER
to read the men's side of the book

The Emotionally Unavailable Man

A Blueprint for Healing

—A Book for Women—

Patti Henry, M.Ed., L.P.C.

Rainbow Books, Inc. ❖ Florida

Library of Congress Cataloging-In-Publication Data

Henry, Patti, 1956-
    The emotionally unavailable man : a blueprint for healing / Patti Henry.
      p. cm.
    Includes index.
    ISBN 1-56825-096-7 (trade softcover : alk. paper)
    1. Men—Psychology. I. Title.
    HQ1090.H46 2004
    158.2—dc22

                                            2004008252

The Emotionally Unavailable Man: A Blueprint for Healing
© 2004 by Patti Henry, M.Ed., L.P.C. (www.patti-henry.com)
ISBN 1-56825-096-7

Published by
    Rainbow Books, Inc., P. O. Box 430, Highland City, FL 33846-0430
Editorial Offices and Wholesale/Distributor Orders
    Telephone: (863) 648-4420
    Email: RBIbooks@aol.com
Individuals' Orders
    Toll-free Telephone (800) 431-1579
    http://www.AllBookStores.com

♾The paper used in this publication meets the minimum requirements of the American National Standard for Information Sciences—Permanence of Paper for Printed Library Materials, ANSI Z39.48–1984.

First edition 2004
10 09 08 07 06 05 04 5 4 3 2 1
Printed in the United States of America

For Jeff

Permissions

Man's Search for Meaning by Viktor Frankl, is published by Beacon Press.

The Onion Field by Joseph Wambaugh, is published by Dell Publishing, a division of Random House, Inc.

The Prophet by Kahlil Gibran, is published by Alfred A. Knopf, a division of Random House, Inc.

"TIME Person of the Year," *TIME*, © 2001 TIME, Inc. Reprinted by permission.

Women's Book Contents

Acknowledgments

Every book has its story. This one goes like this:

I was writing a book when suddenly it occurred to me that I was writing the wrong book. So, I set that manuscript aside, and this one walked in fully intact. Within 15 minutes the complete outline, chapter by chapter, was down on paper. So, first I thank God.

I began writing. With a busy practice, it was hard for me to find the hours I needed to concentrate. So, I set aside 15 hours a week just for this book. I thank my sister and my brother-in-law, Valerie and Kit Carson Smith, who sent me checks for the next six months to pay for those writing hours, so I didn't have to worry about money. Without their financial and emotional backing, this book would not have been possible.

I wrote for four months. My father died. I couldn't concentrate for about six weeks, but when I came back to the manuscript, a new freedom came with me. Somehow I felt my dad's encouragement to write. So, I thank my dad, in a way, for dying. Because in death I believe he received enlightenment and, somehow, that helped me. It reinforced to me how important it was to write this book.

I wrote for two more months. I didn't talk about it much to anyone, but my family quietly supported me: eating lots of take-out, helping with the chores, and not asking how it was going. So, I thank my two boys, Scott and Eric, plus my husband, Jeff, who is my rock, for all their quiet, thorough love, support, and understanding.

Then one day I wrote the last sentence and the last period. I cried.

It was like birthing a baby. I gave my manuscript to my husband with the instructions, "Don't tell me anything negative. Only positives. I can't handle anything negative yet." He honored that. And then we went through it again — and again — and again, each time delving a bit more into honest criticism. He has been my very gentle editor throughout the whole rewriting process. I cannot say thank you enough to him or to God for him.

Next I asked trusted friends, family, and colleagues to read the manuscript and give me feedback, all of which was invaluable. I thank and respectfully acknowledge each of them: my mom and stepfather, Donna and Ernie Holmes; my friends and colleagues: Ruth Arnold, Mona Chamberlain, Woody Forrieter, Karl Weston, Audrey Anastasia, Bill Taube, Susan Herbold, Sylvia Westlake, Bill Clendenen, Joanna Crawford, Wendy Schumer, Heloise Lynn, Fred Crawford, Liz Steele, Amy Gurghigian, Bitsy Cleveland, Kay Schlembach, Michael Marcoux, Ken Bielicki, and Jim Dickinson. Thank you.

Next came the time for the final rewrite and research. For this I received unbelievable amounts of support and encouragement every step along the way. I wish to thank Otto Fad, animal trainer at Sea World in Florida; Bonnie and Troy, assistants at the Houston Civil Court House; Newton Hightower, author of *Anger Busting 101*; and Dr. Reverend Johnny Ray Youngblood, an incredible human being whose energy and belief in me has been life-giving.

Then last, but not least, was my search for a publisher. I must confess, I sent my manuscript to only one: Rainbow Books, Inc. They sent me an offer. We negotiated a bit, wrestled a bit, laughed a bit, and then came to terms. I thank Betty Wright, senior publisher at Rainbow, for being so easy to work with, so full of wisdom, and such a delight.

My acknowledgements would not be complete, however, without mentioning all the clients I have had the honor and privilege to work with over the years. I salute you. I salute your courage. Daily you inspire me and I thank you.

Introduction

I read an astonishing statistic the other day that said that of all the divorces that are filed, over 60 percent of these are filed by women; less than 40 percent by men. I decided to do a little research and find out if this could possibly be true. I went to the Harris County Courthouse which lists all the divorce filings for Houston, Texas, the fourth largest city in America. And guess what? I looked at over 10,000 divorces filed last year and, sure enough, 62 percent of those were filed by women. Almost two-thirds of all the divorces were initiated by the wife!

I pondered this and thought, *Why is that?* I think the answer is two-fold. First, because it's possible. Fifty years ago, when men dominated the workplace, it would not have been possible. One hundred years ago, forget it. But today, it is possible. Women can work. Women can support themselves. In many cases, they can even support their children.

Secondly, because women are in such a position to be able to support themselves, they no longer want to settle for an unfulfilling relationship. I hear women say over and over again, "I want more." "I want a relationship where my husband is emotionally available to me." "I've had enough of talking to a wall." "I've had enough of being ignored." "I've had enough of supporting a man who won't work." "I've had enough of a man who only works." "I've had enough."

If you are such a woman, may this book help you get all the

emotional availability you so crave, seek, and deserve. May it also give you clarity. May it also give you strength.

Chapter 1

Understanding

I will tell you my biases. I am a psychotherapist in private practice. If you come to me for counseling and you are married, I will most likely want to do everything possible to preserve that marriage. If you have children, I will double my efforts. My bias is that I am very pro-marriage. Why? Because marriage seems to be the incubator where wholeness can grow. The irony is, it is also the place where wholeness can be destroyed.

This book is to help you and your partner learn how to create the environment in which the wholeness can grow. The goal is for both people to be happy in the relationship. The goal is for both people — including you — to get their needs met.

In an effort to make that happen, it's important that you know the information provided to your husband/partner. Therefore, you need to read *his* side of the book first. Once you have finished his side of the book, come back and read your side. Your side of the book will make the most sense after you've read his side.

So, at this point, turn the book over and read the men's side of the book. After you have finished, return here to Chapter 2.

Chapter 2

Time to Pause

Take three deep breaths, slowly exhaling. It's time to ponder the other side of this book. I hope you have walked away from it realizing that your partner is a person. He is a wounded, incomplete, imperfect, doesn't-have-a-lot-of-emotional-skills person. He is someone who needs — and deserves — love and kindness in his life. He is somewhat handicapped having had little experience with his emotional self. He's just learning and could use your help in the process.

I hope you walked away from the men's side of the book realizing that he is as much a victim of gender culturalization as you are. I once went to a men's conference led by a dynamic, lovely man. He said that men are getting mixed messages from women. They are being told to "get in touch with their feelings" and at the same time, "Take care of me." They are being told, "Share with me what you are feeling," but also, "Keep me safe." So much of the message is: tell me your feelings but only the ones I want to hear. That is, don't tell me you're scared, don't tell me you feel inadequate, don't tell me you're angry, don't tell me your fears and anxieties, but, tell me your feelings. No wonder men are confused. They are already working in an arena that is fairly unfamiliar to them, and then to have women say, in essence, "edit your feelings" is maddening.

My point is, if you indeed want to have a partner who is emotionally available, then you must make welcome ALL of his emotions, not just the warm and fuzzy ones. You don't get to pick and choose. My question to you is: do you have room for your partner? All of him —

the good and the not so good? Do you have room for his fears and anxieties and inadequacies? Is it safe for him to be a fallible, scared, imperfect human being? And for him to have *needs of his own* separate from yours?

I remember how shocked I was in my own journey with my husband when I realized, "He's just a person." Somehow I had him up high on a pedestal, bigger than life, almost god-like, knowing what to do, having the answers, whole and complete. It was years into our relationship when it occurred to me that *he* felt insecure about things and "less than." I was stunned to realize, "He's just a person."

And I was very distraught. Because suddenly it meant I couldn't be 100 percent safe. It also meant *I* had some responsibility in the system. It meant I had to provide love and safety for *him*. Taking off the rose-colored glasses, the knight in shining armor fiction, and making room for all of your partner, begins the process of making it safe for him to be emotionally available to you.

And that's what we want.

Chapter 3

Things You Can Do

This chapter almost has to start with what you can't do in order to get to what you can. Why? Because women historically have been taught to do, do, do. Give, give, give. People please. Keep the peace. Be nice. Don't hurt people's feelings. What messages were *you* given? This is the first thing you can do: examine those messages. This is the first thing you can't do: accept them all as Truths and how to be in the world.

Were you taught to be a caretaker? To give, to give, to give some more. To take the burnt pork chop at dinner leaving the good ones for everyone else. To sit in the hard chair leaving the comfortable chairs for your husband and kids. To buy the gifts. To write the thank you notes. To keep track of people's birthdays. To plan the luncheons. To give, to give, to give.

Were you taught to be tenacious in relationships? To try, to try again, and then to try some more? Were you taught not to give up? To be loyal. To put up with way too much. Were you taught no matter what to stand by your man? How about the Cinderella stories? Were you taught that you were the princess and Prince Charming would someday be along to meet your every need — not having any needs of his own, of course?

This book is not about giving more or trying harder. It is about learning to give differently. Maybe WAY differently than you were taught. If you water a plant and water and water and water it when it really needs to be allowed to dry out between waterings, the plant will

die. More is not better — it's lethal. The question is: are the messages you were taught growing up a female in our society helpful, or are you killing the plant? Are they even accurate? Do you believe them? Do you want your life to be ruled by them or are you ready for a change?

In AA there is this wonderful saying about meetings: take what you like and leave the rest. So it is with the messages you were taught: take what you like and leave the rest. In other words, it's time for you to discard messages you were taught that don't work. That cause you pain. That are absurd. This is step #1.

Self-Define

The second thing you can do in order to change the dynamics in your relationship and encourage emotional availability is to self-define. This is no different than what I tell men on the other side of this book. You've got to have a self. You've got to take the time for self-introspection and find out who you really are. What you think, what you feel, what you like, what you hate, what you stand for, what's fun for you, what's sacred, what holds you back. Often what gets in the way of this process for women is codependency. So, the second thing you can do is self-define. The second thing you cannot do is get sucked into codependency.

Codependency

Codependency is the antithesis of self-definition. It doesn't allow it. Remember in a healthy relationship there are three complete, whole entities: a whole "I", a whole "you", and a whole "us." Codependency focuses only on the "us" or in extreme cases, only on the "you" (that is, the man in your life). It does not encourage, or even have room for, an "I." It is what I call getting lost in a relationship. It is certainly having an over-reaction to things outside of us (what's he thinking? what's he doing? what's he feeling?) and an under-reaction to things

inside ourselves (how am *I* doing?). It's when our relationship becomes our LIFE. It's when we give way too much power to what he says and does. It's when my worth is determined by him. Obsessive thinking about him — what he's doing or needs to do — takes over my life.

Another red flag of codependency is when his likes determine my likes. That is, if he likes motorcycles, I can like motorcycles. If he likes stamp collecting, I can like stamp collecting. If he likes music and plays in a band, I can learn to play an instrument, too. It is somewhat like being a chameleon. The behavior says, whatever you want me to be, I'll be. However you need for me to be so you'll love me, I'll be that. Again, this is not having a clear self-definition.

Relationships work best when both people know themselves. This includes you. Relationships work best when both people are clear that they are capable of taking care of themselves. This includes you. I cannot tell you how many, many single women I have worked with who at 30 or 33 or even 35, were still living in apartments. Now, each of these women had good jobs with good salaries. When I asked them why they were throwing their money away instead of building up equity in a home, each looked at me blankly. It had never even occurred to them that they could buy a house *without a man*. And that they needed to! It never occurred to them to be financially responsible to *themselves*. Instead, each was waiting to get married and THEN she would buy a house. In the meantime, apartments were loving them: all that rent with no obligation of return.

The point is, whether you are married or single, you cannot wait to have a self. You cannot wait for some man to come into your life to define you. You must define yourself. Conversely, you cannot wait for your husband to get self-defined before you define yourself. Life is short. You can't wait for him to get it before you give yourself permission to. It's sort of like saying, "I'll have healthy behavior when he does." You cannot wait for him to have healthy behavior. He may never have healthy behavior. You, nonetheless, need to.

"Fixing" Him

Another red flag of codependency is when you are trying to "fix" your partner. Now, I am 100 percent for healing your partner, but fixing is a different story. What's the difference? Healing comes from understanding your partner's wounds and making it safe enough for his growth to occur. Fixing is doing the work for him. Doing the thinking, the figuring out, looking at all the options, and then telling him what he needs to do.

This is not helpful. This will not make an emotionally unavailable man emotionally available. It is not good for you either. It keeps you from looking at your own stuff. This kind of codependency not only stunts your husband's growth, but yours as well. Self-esteem and self-empowerment come from "I can do it myself." If we do for our partner — or our kids for that matter — what he needs to be doing on his own, we rob him of the victory HE needs. And, if we do for our partner what he needs to be doing on his own, we don't have the time or energy to do what WE need to be doing for our own victories. What part of you do you need to develop? If you stop putting your energies into HIM, who will you be?

Now, I am not advocating parallel lives either. Parallel lives is where you have your life, and he has his life, and you live under the same roof rather as roommates. You see each other every once in a while, eat together sometimes, have sex together on occasion, go to company functions as needed, but you basically are not journeying together.

So I know what you're thinking: this is clear as mud. On the one hand I'm saying develop a self and don't make him your "project," while on the other hand I'm saying stay connected and don't have parallel lives. And the answer is: do both. You must develop the whole "I," make it safe for your partner to develop the whole "you," and then stay connected to — but not swallowed up by — the whole "us." Having an "us" does not mean not having an "I" and a "you." Having an "I" does not mean not having an "us." As Dr. Seuss says, life's a great balancing act. So it is in relationships. The caution is to keep the three entities in balance and not to let one obscure the rest.

Family of Origin

The third thing you can do to help your partner in his emotional growth process is to become aware of why you are with someone who is emotionally unavailable in the first place. This includes looking at your family of origin (FOO) as well as looking at your secondary gains. What we don't get resolved in our childhood, in our FOO, we bring into our marriage. Makes sense. Where else would it go? Of course we bring our unresolved junk in the hopes of getting these issues resolved. Most of this process happens subconsciously.

For example, if I have an emotionally unavailable parent, chances are I'll marry an emotionally unavailable partner. And doesn't that sound crazy? Who would do that? The answer is: we all do. Our sub-conscious wants us to be whole so badly that it will help us fall in love with someone who will help recreate our unresolved history in the hopes that it will come out differently this time. This recreation happens on an emotional level. That is, we are usually conscious enough to not repeat the exact same pattern.

For example, if I was poor growing up, I might marry someone with a really good income. However, he might be so tight with the purse strings, that I end up FEELING impoverished. Or, if my father was a traveling salesman and was gone all the time, I probably won't marry a traveling salesman who is gone all the time. I might look for the exact opposite. I might marry a man who is home for dinner every night by 6:00. However, it turns out he may be a man who doesn't like to talk. We spend most of our evenings in silence. Or the man I marry is home every night but gets stoned as soon as he walks in the door. Or he loves to tinker with engines and so, even though he's home, he's in the garage for hours working on his boat or fixing up used cars to sell. Or he likes to read and always has his nose in a good book. Or he turns on the TV the moment he walks in the door. There are a thousand scenarios, but they all come back to the same thing: like my dad, or like my mom, or both, my husband isn't really "there for me."

It is important you become aware of this so you can know what it

is that your husband needs to heal inside of *you*. It will help him be less defended as well as help him get clear about his own healing power and how important that is in your marriage. It will also allow you to understand why you are in the relationship in the first place. You can stop beating yourself up about it. You can give yourself grace. You can be kinder to yourself knowing it has been your subconscious at work. It can help you make sense out of your behavior and also give you a starting point to begin to work with your husband to change it.

Searching For a Diagnosis

It's rather like getting a disease or illness diagnosed. If we aren't feeling well in general or we have a sharp recurring pain or our right hand goes numb or whatever, we go to the doctor hoping he/she can find the problem. We want an answer. We want a diagnosis. We want to know *what* is wrong so we can know *how* to treat it. There's nothing more frustrating than going from doctor to doctor with an ailment that you know is real and being told, "We can't find anything." And what I'm telling you in your relationship is that *emotionally* we CAN find something. I can tell you — definitively — that if you are with an emotionally unavailable man, that it is in your history somewhere. Once you find it, identify it, there is your diagnosis and now you can know what needs to be healed. You have a starting point.

Sometimes it's a little tricky to see. I'll ask a woman who obviously has emotional unavailability somewhere in her history because she's married to a man who travels six months out of the year and works 14 hour days, seven days a week the other six months, and she will say, "No, my parents were both available to me. My father was home every night. My mother was always there." When I press and ask if her father was emotionally there for her, often I get with a laugh, "Oh, no, not emotionally. No way!" Still, there's no connection for her. At this point I gently say, "Well, that's the parallel." And *then* it clicks for her. Then she can see it. Then she understands it's a wound she's been carrying, and at some level, recreating with her partner.

Crazy as it sounds, we recreate it subconsciously in order to have the opportunity to have the wound HEALED.

Our Subconscious

Our minds are so complex. I am often totally in awe of our subconscious processes. But this much I know is true: we have subconscious processes. And we must become aware of them in order to do the necessary healing. I liken it to snorkeling. The first time I went snorkeling was in Cancun on the fourth day of a four day holiday. For three days, I just enjoyed Cancun so much. The water was beautiful, the beaches were beautiful, the sunsets were beautiful. It was just lovely. Then, on day four, my friend and I decided to rent masks and go snorkeling. I will never forget the *moment* I put that mask to the water. I was STUNNED. The brightly colored gorgeous fish and coral I saw were amazing! Now, I had seen Jacques Cousteau specials on TV when I grew up. I had seen aquariums at the zoo and fish in fish tanks at the pet store. But to be surrounded by such marine life, to see the brilliance of the color, to watch whole schools of fish swim by — was astonishing. Then it occurred to me. The most astonishing fact of all was that the day before *it hadn't existed*. Well, yes, of course it did. But, to me, the day before, it hadn't existed. I had no conscious awareness of it. I had no connection to it.

That's how our subconscious works. Yes, of course it exists. It's there. It's always been there. But until you get connected to it, it's as if it isn't there at all. So, look in your family of origin to identify where that emotional unavailability was that you have duplicated in your marriage. It's there. I assure you. You just have to put your mask on and see it. And, by the way, once you are able to see it, it will almost smack you in the face. Suddenly you will be able to see it and see it clearly. It's rather like one of those pictures that has a picture within it. You have to stare at it, and then, in one *instant,* you can see clearly the hidden picture.

To Review a Bit

In understanding what you can — and can't — do to encourage your husband's emotional healing and growth, you must first take a look at yourself. Examine the messages you were given growing up, and figure out which ones work for you and which ones to discard. Second, you need to self-define and fend off codependency. Third, you need to be able to see WHY you are with an emotionally unavailable man from a family of origin point of view. Next, you'll want to look at why you are with an emotionally unavailable man from a secondary gains point of view.

Secondary Gains

What are secondary gains? Secondary gains are hidden benefits we derive from our behavior. We are not actively, consciously seeking these particular benefits, but we get them nonetheless. They are not always positive. Sometimes we are not even aware that we are getting them.

For example, let's say your elderly mother is in a nursing home and you complain about having to visit her daily. It's time consuming. She doesn't appreciate it. It's unpleasant. You hate it. This is where secondary gains come in. People will not continue a behavior unless they are getting something out of it. In this case, your secondary gains include: You get to feel good about yourself. Look at all the sacrifice you're making. You're such a good daughter. Also, others see you as a saint. You get praise from your family. You get praise from the nursing home staff. Everyone knows you there on a first name basis. You get to feel important. Not to mention it gets you out of having to have sex with your husband. Clearly you're too exhausted for THAT. It keeps him at a distance which is fine with you because then you don't really have to put time and energy into him. These are secondary gains. Somehow you get to feel good about yourself — or even bad about yourself — and, most importantly, you get to avoid something.

What are your secondary gains in your marriage/relationship? Why

do you keep staying with someone who is emotionally unavailable? Why do you settle? What do you do to encourage the system to stay the same? and why? The 'why' is important because it can help you identify your secondary gains. And there are LOTS of possibilities. Here are some of the more frequently cited secondary gains involved in keeping the system the same that I hear in my sessions:

- I'm not the problem. He is.
- I feel superior.
- I like to beat him up. It sounds sick, but I enjoy it. It feels good to belittle him.
- I really don't have to do any work on myself.
- It makes me feel bad about myself, and that feels normal.
- It allows me to once again not get my needs met, and that feels normal.
- I don't have to go into the fear. I know this pattern. I don't have to risk.
- People feel sorry for me. I actually get a lot of attention from other people because he's not there for me.
- I can feel sorry for me. And I can justify buying things (or eating things, or having affairs, etc.).
- I get to feel miserable. I don't know what it's like to feel good. It's a habit, I guess. Miserable is safe. At least I'm never disappointed.
- Yelling gives me an adrenalin rush.
- I don't have to have sex.
- I can be self-righteous and I like that.
- I don't have to risk being known at any deep level. I don't have to be vulnerable.
- I get money out of him. If I ask more from him, he might leave me and then I'll have no money.

The list goes on and on. Get honest with yourself. What are your secondary gains? Believe me, they are there. Otherwise, you would have left the relationship a long time ago. Remember, your goal is to help your partner in his emotional growth process in order to be able to get your needs met. To be happy. To be whole. To create a win/win situation. You must become aware of your secondary gains and honestly confront them in order to make this possible. For often, it is exactly the secondary gains that encourage emotional unavailability, and *prevent* emotional availability in our partners. If your highest truth is that you want your partner to be emotionally available to you so that you both can be whole and happy — and I believe that it is — then you must address your secondary gains.

Boundaries

Next, as in the men's half of this book, you must have boundaries. Boundaries are like lines: on one side it feels good, on the other side it feels bad. If you are feeling bad about something, that means you haven't had a boundary. And you need one. Boundaries are completely, 100 percent your responsibility. Nobody has to "let you" have them. You don't need anyone's permission. You don't need anyone's encouragement or telling you it's okay. If you're in a bad place about something, YOU need to get clear where your line is. What would feel good to you and what feels bad. I hear a lot of victim responses to this. I hear a lot of whiney, childlike responses to this. "I TRY to have a boundary and he doesn't respect it." "He won't let me have a boundary." "It doesn't do any good to have a boundary. He just ignores it." I can almost hear my eight year old protesting his older brother's winning the game, stomping his foot and crying, "It's not fair!"

We all regress to child behavior on occasion. That's normal so be gentle with yourself. What I'm saying, however, is, as far as boundaries go, you must learn to stay in your adult. The equation is simple: if anything you are doing or saying feels bad, feels wrong, you don't have an appropriate boundary — and you need one. You are not a

victim. Do not say yes when the answer is no or no when the answer is yes. Get rid of any idea you may carry that a boundary has anything to do with the other person. It only has to do with you. It only has to do with this feels good to me, and this doesn't. Boundaries are very personal. And *you are responsible* for yours. No one else is. You are.

Remember, too, boundaries without consequences are worthless. If someone doesn't "respect" your boundary, it's because either you haven't made it clear or you haven't had a consequence for when someone crossed over your line.

I worked with one woman whose husband went through her admittedly overcrowded closet and gave away her clothes to charity. This infuriated her. This made her crazy. But at a deeper level it felt extremely violating, almost like emotional rape to her. And yet it kept happening. I asked her where is your boundary? Is it okay that he does that? She was able to say quite clearly that no, it was NOT okay with her and that it felt excruciatingly violating. She came from poverty where she had nothing, and for her husband to give her things away without her permission was intolerable. Which makes sense. What had she done about it so far? "I've told him over and over again not to do that!" What was her consequence? She would get angry, she would get hurt. Sometimes cry, sometimes hurricane. Was it working? Of course it wasn't. Her husband's behavior continued to be the same. I asked her to get CLEAR what her boundary was and what she was willing to do to keep it in tact. Now, there's no one answer. There are lots of possibilities. She brainstormed and came up with several options.

First of all, she realized her closet was overstuffed and it made sense to her why her husband was distressed about it. She looked at whether her behavior was passive aggressive anger (underground anger) toward her husband and she decided it was not. Instead, it represented her fear of not having. For her own personal growth and to help her husband feel heard, she decided to work on cleaning it out. But, she also decided that she did not want her husband's help or intervention in it.

She sat down calmly and explained all this to him. She let him know how violating it had felt in the past. She let him know how dif-

ficult the task was for her, because she had had so little growing up that her tendency was to hold onto everything. She told him it would not be acceptable to her AT ALL should he give her things away again without her permission. For this she was willing to go to the mat. Her words, "If you do this to me again, I will seriously have to consider whether I want to continue to live with someone who repeatedly violates me at such a deep level. Do you understand? This CANNOT happen again."

By taking responsibility for making her boundary clear plus deciding for herself what her consequence would be, she was able to change the pattern she was in with her husband. Together they implemented a win/win solution: she cleaned out her closet which gave her husband some relief, and he did not intervene which gave her a feeling of personal power and the victory she needed as she got through a difficult task.

No one can run over you unless you let them. If you are letting them, you need a boundary. Figure out your line. Take responsibility to set it in place and enforce it. It is a simple concept but also one that takes a lot of practice to master. Don't worry if you bungle along for a while when you are figuring out boundaries. Keep practicing.

Red Flags

I've noticed three red flag areas where women, in particular, need to be extra careful about boundaries. The first, as stated above, is letting people run over them all the while stomping their feet crying, "Not fair!" To change this, you must get out of your child ego state and into your adult. Take responsibility.

The second red flag area is when women get stuck in the "doing too much" place. The martyr syndrome. Saying yes, saying yes, saying yes yet again. Adjusting. Taking on more. Not exercising the word, "No." Or, "No, that won't work for me." Avoiding conflict. Being "nice." Trying not to hurt anyone's feelings. Trying to please everyone every time.

This is cultural and family of origin training. If you feel like you're drowning under too much pressure, too many obligations, too much to get done — then you don't have good boundaries. Again, it's not anything or anyone outside of you. It's you. It's your raising your hand saying, "Okay, I'll do it." It's you who is thinking, "If I don't do it, it won't get done." It's you being dishonest with yourself at some level: believing you are the only one who can save the day.

Where are your lines? When is enough enough? If things don't get done, they don't get done. The moon has yet to fall out of the sky. Let some of it go. Learn the magic and the power of "No." Learn the magic and power of delegating. Of course, you'll also have to be willing to let go of secondary gains. Saying yes does make us important, but do you feel on a regular basis, "Everyone thinks I'm wonderful, but I'm dying. I can't do this anymore!" That's a sure indication of poor boundaries. You are responsible to change that. No one else is going to put up boundaries for you. YOU have to do it. Sorry, but it's true. You have to be the one to practice saying no and setting limits.

Talking Too Much

A third red flag area for women is talking too much. Not only talking too much, but telling too much. First of all, talking relentlessly in a relationship is not helpful. It takes up too much room. There has to be room for your partner as well. If you talk 90 percent of the time you are doing the work for both of you. Talk less. Make room for your partner. If there are silences, that's okay. If there are only silences, that's a different story. That's emotional unavailability, and that's not okay. Try to find a good balance where there is space for both of you. I met a woman once who talked fast and almost non-stop. It was hard to get a word in edgewise. She told me she was divorced. It turns out her husband had left her because she talked too much — which she found amusing. I found believable. Seems she missed a most valuable lesson.

What about telling too much? Sharing very personal thoughts and feelings with people you hardly know is telling too much. Sharing

things with other people that were told to you in confidence is telling too much. Sharing the arguments and discussions you have with your partner with friends and family is telling too much. All indicate poor boundaries. All indicate a need for boundaries.

You have a right to privacy. That means you do not have to tell everything to everybody. If you have that feeling of needing to "tell all," you have a boundary problem. This often comes from an insecurity, a fear of not being liked. A belief that people will not like you when you talk less, tell less. The irony is they will probably like and respect you MORE when you learn to respect your own right to privacy. People with poor boundaries who tell too much make people with clear boundaries nervous. After all, if you talk to me about others, you will talk to others about me. Therefore, I'm not as likely to open up to you on a deeper level. It's not safe. Good boundaries make it safe. Deeper friendships can develop.

So far there have been four things you can do to help your husband become more emotionally available:

1. Examine the family of origin messages you carry around — keep what you like and discard the rest.
2. Self-define and fend off codependency.
3. Get honest with yourself about why you stay with an emotionally unavailable man. Look at family of origin. Look at secondary gains.
4. Develop better boundaries.

These are all personal growth issues. These are things you need to do for yourself whether or not you are in a relationship. The next couple of steps pertain to your partner more directly. They will help you claim your adult self and your own personal power.

Rose-Colored Glasses

First, take off the rose-colored glasses. Here you must look at your partner and your marriage more realistically. This is exceedingly difficult for some women to do. We want our partners to be adults who will *take care of us*. At least emotionally. Keep us safe. Handle things. Be loving. Romance would be great. Understand us. And as one of my clients said to her husband, "I just want you to adore me." Now, I think this is normal. We each have a little part inside of us that wants to remain a child. In fact, this is one of the basic tenants of Judeo Christianity that makes it so attractive: that we are all as children with a Father who will take care of us. A Father who will love us no matter what and comfort us and give us hope. A Father who will understand even when we pout like a two year old because things didn't go our way.

So it is in our marriage: we long for our partner to care for us in such a way. The problem with this is two-fold. First of all, your partner isn't God. God doesn't have any needs. Your partner does. Second, your partner longs for the same thing you do: for you to be an adult and take care of *him*. At least emotionally. To be kept safe. For you to handle things. Be loving. Romance him, understand him, and adore him.

This is somewhat of a secret in our society: men hide it away. But, I tell you this, after working with hundreds and hundreds of men individually, it is true. In the quiet moments when they feel really safe, they talk about that little piece of themselves. That piece that wants to remain a child, not be responsible, be taken care of. Again, I think that's normal. It seems to be a piece of the human psyche. What's not "normal" is for us, as women and as a society, to pretend that part isn't there. Men need to be nurtured and loved, too. Supported. Believed in. They are no different than you and me in this regard.

Seeing the Wounds

Another part of taking off the rose-colored glasses is coming to terms with the incompleteness and woundedness of your partner. Be-

cause none of us is perfect, none of us got perfect parenting. There is ALWAYS incompleteness and wounding in childhood. If your partner is emotionally unavailable, we can conclude there was a significant amount of incompleteness and wounding in his past. No one becomes emotionally unavailable for fun, for no reason, on a whim, etc. Emotional unavailability comes from emotional damage. The wounding happened long before your husband met you. So it's not your fault. But you must get, the wounding *did happen*.

Therefore, taking off the rose-colored glasses means beginning to see your husband more kindly, with more compassion. He was hurt as a child. He's not emotionally unavailable to you on purpose. He doesn't know how to do it differently. Of course, he has to learn, but being able to see the wounds your partner carries can help you be more patient with his process. More tender. This tenderness, this seeing beyond the surface, will help him heal. And remember, the more you can help him heal, the faster he can become emotionally available to you.

It Is Not About You

Also, being able to see your husband's incompleteness and woundedness can be a wonderful way to learn how not to take things personally. Most of the time when he is acting out or pulling into his defended self, IT IS NOT ABOUT YOU. It is about his wound. This is a very abstract concept that is difficult for many people to understand.

When your partner is being withdrawn from you, being mean to you, being inconsiderate of you, being reactionary toward you, it is difficult to believe that IT IS NOT ABOUT YOU. But it's not. Well, it might be about you a *little* bit: you may be the trigger to his wound or incompleteness. I think in terms of it is 10 percent now (the trigger) and 90 percent history (the wound). So, if you can say to yourself when he is acting out, "This is not about me. I'm the trigger, but this is not about me. It's bigger than me. This is about his woundedness or incompleteness," it will help you not feel hurt. Yes, he's directing it toward you, but, no, it is not about you. If you can see his wound, you

can stay out of your hurt. If you can stay out of your hurt, you can help him.

But remember, you've got to have boundaries. Know that when he is reactionary it is not about you, but you do need to respond to him by drawing appropriate lines to take care of yourself. You are not a victim. Don't act like one. Next, with your boundaries in place, practice responding with tenderness and genuine caring toward your husband instead of hurricaning or punishing him. And finally, remember to always work to create win/win solutions.

Chapter 4

Making It Safe

I believe marriage is about healing: that the whole purpose of marriage is to heal each other into wholeness. Therefore, it's your job to heal your husband. And it's his job to heal you. Of course there are exceptions to this rule which we'll discuss in Chapter 7, but besides the exceptions, healing ought to be both of yours goal.

Healing works best when it is a mutual act. That is, you work on healing your husband while he works on healing you: at the same time. You cannot wait until he heals you to start healing him. You cannot wait until his side of the street is clean before you start cleaning yours. Why? Because it doesn't work. He needs *your* healing power in order to be able to thoroughly clean his side of the street. Of course, the reverse is true, too. You need *his* healing power to get your side of the street completely clean. Therefore, mutual healing is the goal.

Making it safe involves mutuality. I take care of you, you take care of me. I heal you, you heal me. Mutuality builds trust. It lets me know I'm not hanging out there all by myself but that you're willing to hang, too. I'm willing to be vulnerable if you are, and you are if I am. That's how this country was formed. Think of our U.S. Declaration of Independence. Fifty-six men decided to sign a most treasonous document that would lead to their sure deaths if the revolution was not successful. Each supported the other in their courage by being willing to sign *their own names* to it. Thus it is in building safety in your relationship.

You have to be willing to mutually, fully participate in the commitment to healing your partner and *allowing him to heal you*. That's

the vulnerability part. You engage in healing your partner while, at the same time, you allow him to heal you. You cannot focus only on healing him and refuse any healing offered to you. It has to be a mutual act. Otherwise, one or the other of you will feel too vulnerable, too naked, too exposed. Very few people would feel comfortable standing completely naked in a group of people where everyone else is completely clothed. With our partner, it's like that. It's a trust issue. If I'm going to expect you to be vulnerable with me, I must be willing to be vulnerable, too.

Working Together

Working together in this mutual healing is learning to use the resources you have available: each other. It reminds me of a story I once was told about the difference between Heaven and Hell. In Hell, there is a long banquet table where everyone is seated. In front of each person is a huge bowl of rich, scrumptious soup. And yet everyone sitting there is starving . They are emaciated, withered, depressed. The problem turns out to be that their soup spoons are four feet long, and therefore, they can't get the soup to their mouths. In visiting Heaven, we see the same scenario. Everyone in a banquet hall at long tables with soup in front of them and four foot-long soup spoons. But in this picture, everyone is happy, round, well-fed. How is this possible one might ask? It turns out in Heaven, the people used their spoons to *feed each other*. Thus it is in marriage. We must learn to feed each other, to heal each other, to give and to receive.

Physical Safety

The foundation that makes healing possible is emotional safety. Not to state the obvious, but, a person cannot feel emotionally safe without physical safety first. Therefore, if you are engaged in any physical abuse of your partner, that is the first thing that you have to ad-

dress. Hitting, kicking, biting, scratching, slapping must cease. No exceptions. These are the obvious forms of physical abuse. Some less obvious ways of being physically abusive are throwing things, hitting with objects, ripping the covers off your partner as he's sleeping, ripping his clothes, spitting on him, threatening him with a gun or knife. Any action that violates the person's body or physical space feels violent to the receiver. And, of course, violence will never create emotional safety. It will destroy it.

Furthermore, a little bit goes a long way toward that end. If you spend months creating an emotionally safe environment and then have one night of physical abuse, you have just destroyed all that trust you were building up. Which leads to a word about addictions.

Addictions

Addictions, especially to alcohol or any other drug which chemically alters you, own you. You no longer get to be in charge of your life or behavior because the chemical is in charge. Chemicals can not — and do not — create emotional safety for our partners. People do. If you have an addiction, you *will not be able to* provide emotional safety for your partner or for your children, until you get sober. Period. No exceptions. You may *think* you are providing emotional safety, but your chemical is talking to you. Chemicals lie; they don't tell the truth. In fact, addiction is the only disease that lies to you and says there is no problem when there is a problem. If you get bronchitis, your body tells you, "Hey! There's a problem here!" If you get diabetes your body tells you, "Attention! Something's wrong!" Or MS or Parkinson's disease or even a sprained ankle or a tiny splinter. Your body talks to you and says, "Listen, there's a problem you need to look at."

With addiction, your body LIES to you. It says, "I don't have a problem. I'm not over the line. Everything's fine." It is the chemical talking. Now, the only way to stop the chemical from talking is to get the chemical out of your body. There is a saying in the anonymous programs (AA,CA,NA,GA,etc.) about sobriety: sobriety is getting clean

with yourself. To me that means not just getting honest with yourself but also CLEAN of your chemicals. Clean out your sacred body.

If you have an addiction or even think you *might*, get help. If you have enough money to go to a therapist, go to one. If not, go to a 12-step program (they are free). The ideal is to do both. The main thing is to realize that if your goal is a great relationship with your partner where you both feel happy and free and powerful and safe, you must get sober to get there. Addiction is not your friend, not your ally, in meeting your goal. It's so obvious it's almost embarrassing to talk about. I don't want to insult your intelligence. But it's like having an empty swimming pool and everyday longing to swim. Well, duh. Fill up the pool! It's that obvious: if you have an addiction you cannot provide emotional safety. Get sober — get the chemical out of your life — and you can.

Hurricaning

Raging — hurricaning — is addictive. It chemically alters your body. It pumps in tons of adrenalin so you can actually get a rush or a high. Maybe you don't identify it as such, but your body dramatically chemically changes during this process. People often describe to me being able to feel the chemicals pumping in. Then, after the hurricane, they often crash into exhaustion. Which makes sense from a chemical point of view. It's like being in a car crash where we have a sudden surge of adrenalin and then feel wiped out after it's all over. If you are raging at your partner on a regular basis — hurricaning — you are actually experiencing a drug addiction. And, like alcohol or cocaine or marijuana or Xanax, adrenalin addiction is destructive, not only to your marriage, but to your body. Some people call it the Type A personality where a person is explosive, short-fused, intense. Study after study shows these people have more heart attacks, more strokes, more accidents.

So, from a purely selfish angle, you need to stop hurricaning because it hurts your body. In the bigger picture, it hurts your marriage and your children. Remember, someone who is chemically altered can-

not provide emotional safety. The chemical, though self-produced, is in charge. Furthermore, your husband will not be able to be emotionally available to you if he does not feel safe. When I work with couples the wife is often shocked at how much her husband will share in sessions. That tells me three things. First, he doesn't share as openly at home, and second, he doesn't feel safe enough to do so. Lastly, it tells me that IF safety is provided he will be able to be more available to his wife. The bottom line for me in all my sessions is "create safety." Thus it needs to be in your home. My clients know I'm not going to hurricane on them. They know I'm not going to judge them or beat them up emotionally. They know there is a space for them to talk without being told they are wrong. Does your partner know these things about you?

Giving Up Control

Raging/hurricaning is a way of being controlling. If you keep your partner in a state of trauma, he, like the rest of us, will do just about anything to stop the pain. Now, I'm not suggesting that all women openly rage as their way of hurricaning. Any hint of relentlessness can be hurricaning. Any hint of rigidity, non-flexibility can be hurricaning. Taking up all the space because you know best can be, from your husband's point of view, hurricaning. It's, at least, controlling.

To stop this pattern in your relationship and help your husband heal, YOU HAVE TO CHANGE. You can't treat him the same, and expect different results. If you treat him the same, you are going to continue to get emotional unavailability.

Comfort Zones

One change you have to make in changing the system is giving yourself permission to be more vulnerable. This is extremely scary for many, many people. I'm going to assume you are one of them, because we attract people at the same level of healthiness, and you are with an

emotionally unavailable man. What that means is, we attract people at the same level of being able to tolerate emotional connections.

Let's say there is a scale from 1 to 100 and everyone is a number. The higher your number, the more emotional connections you can tolerate and the more you can allow yourself to be vulnerable. So, if you are a 62, chances are you attract and are attracted to other 62s. That is, someone who is an 88 on the scale — who can tolerate LOTS of emotional connection — is not going to date a 20, someone who has a low tolerance for emotional connections. It wouldn't be satisfying enough for the 88. Conversely, a 31 is NOT going to date a 67 because that would be just way too scary for them. It would feel invasive, suffocating, way, way, way too vulnerable. So, 20s date 20s, 70s date 70s, 8s usually don't date, and 95s are not reading this book. Why? Because they are married to people who are 95s and can tolerate lots of connection, vulnerability, and emotional availability. P.S. 95s are rare.

So, whatever your arbitrary number, your partner's number is close to yours. In order to increase your number and make it safe for your partner to increase his number, you have to increase your willingness to be vulnerable. And, I assure you, this will feel out of control. It will feel a bit like jumping off a cliff into water below hoping you are going to live through the experience. It will feel like free-falling from a plane, hoping your parachute opens. Here's a diagram if your number is 53:

Step 1

This is my comfort zone. I feel comfortable here and know what to expect (even if it's bad).

Step 2

I want to get to #58 (more connection /intimacy tolerance), but those 5 extra connections are OUTSIDE of my comfort zone. When I'm in this 5-point stretch outside of my comfort zone, I feel scared, I feel out of control. I often run back to #53 behavior. I want to quit. I want to stay in 53

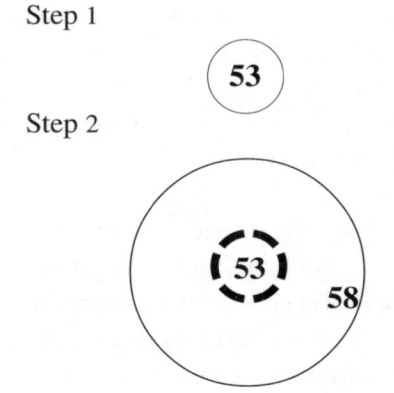

which I know and feel comfortable in. I feel SO vulnerable. This step takes a long time — days at least, sometimes weeks, sometimes months.

Step 3

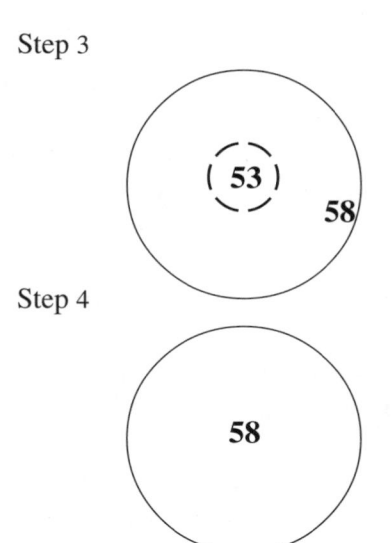

I have tolerated my additional vulnerability and fear, and now I can easily flow back and forth from 53 to 58. It is still scary sometimes, but I'm getting more and more used to 54, 55, 56, 57, and 58 behavior.

Step 4

My comfort zone has expanded. I am now a 58, and it feels good. I am not scared anymore of this increased connection and vulnerability. I'm enjoying it. I am comfortable here.

My point is, to help your partner become more emotionally available to you, YOU have to be willing to be more emotionally available, too. This means letting go of the feeling of being in control and stepping into territory that's outside your comfort zone. This often means speaking more kindly, more lovingly, sweeter if you will. Getting the edge out of your voice or the attitude. Responding rather than reacting. Being more honest with your partner, but in a gentle way. Living in personal integrity: not doing things that, when examined, you know would be harmful to your partner's emotional safety.

It means learning how to stop throwing poisonous darts at your partner even when he shoots one at you. Instead, respond with a boundary that is loving and kind, "You know, I will not accept being talked to that way. I deserve to be talked to with respect. I am committed to making our marriage better and (here is the stretch outside your comfort zone — here is the free-fall) and I know you are, too. I can see all

the efforts you've been making, and they are so nice. Don't think I don't notice because I do. We have to just keep working at speaking kinder to each other." You'll probably get an apology — if not now, later. Create safety for your partner by being vulnerable enough to make it safe for him. By being gentle, being kind.

Tell the Truth

Another way to create safety in your relationship is by being willing to speak the truth out loud. By being in personal integrity. Tell the truth. Be honest. If you are hiding things (credit card debt, new purchases, the fact that you quit your job, your unhappiness, etc.), how can *safety* come from that?

If you hide things because your husband is explosive, you must get willing to say that out loud. Again, in as kind a way as you can. With a loving voice. "You know I love you. You know I'm committed to making our marriage wonderful. So, in order to do that I have to be able to talk to you even about the hard stuff. My problem is, I'm afraid to do that. Maybe I learned that as a child growing up with my mother always screaming, I don't know. But I do know (and here's the stretch, here's the free-fall) that in the depths of my heart, you are a good man. Now hear me out. Really, I think you're wonderful. But I also think that you learned somewhere to explode when you are angry. I BE-LIEVE that when you do that you are not trying to hurt me. Is that right? I feel like your heart is in the right place, but you just get reactionary. So, this is the part I really need you to hear: your explosiveness scares me. It shuts me down. I can't even talk. It actually keeps me from opening up to you which I know is EXACTLY what you don't want. I want this pattern to change. I'm willing to do whatever I can to help. Are you willing to work on your explosiveness?"

You must get willing to talk about the hard stuff. You must get willing to say the truth out loud. Take a deep breath and plunge. Let your honesty be gentle, but let your honesty BE.

Codes

This means learning how to let go of speaking in codes, as well. That is, learning how to be more direct with important information. Here is an example you might recognize yourself in. Your partner has just said or done something really hurtful to you. Or maybe he hasn't done or said something he needed to, and that's hurtful to you. You feel yourself pull in and shut down. Then he says, to add insult to injury, "What's wrong?" Your response? A terse, "Nothing." That's a code. Of course something's wrong! At this point your husband can either take your word for it, "Ok, nothing's wrong," or he can feel lied to because he KNOWS what you are saying isn't true. Neither interpretation of your, "Nothing," lends itself to creating safety in your relationship. Not for you, not for him. Not speaking in code may sound something like this, "I'm hurt and I'm not able to talk to you about it right now. I will talk to you about it as soon as I can. Please leave me alone right now."

I hear codes ALL THE TIME in therapy sessions. A common one is, "I want a divorce." I ask, *"Do* you want a divorce, or do you want your marriage to be different?" Inevitably the answer is: I want my marriage to be different. I say, "Then say that!" Take care with your words. Make sure what you are saying is TRUE. So often the code is, "I hate you! Go away!" when the truthful experience is: "I love you and I want you to love me. What you are doing is HURTING me — please STOP it. Love me."

I had a 17-year-old girl tell her mother in a session, "My home is not safe for me. You've got to stop Dad from pulling the rug out from under me all the time. I won't live that way anymore. If you are not willing to commit to protecting me, I am going to move out of the house." And she meant it.

Her mother's response? "Well, you'd never make it. You still need us financially. You can't pay your car insurance. How could you ever pay rent?" I was incredulous. I realized she was speaking in code, and the decode was, "I don't want you to leave." I asked the mother if that was what she was really saying, and as her tears came to her, she said,

"Yes." She then told her daughter how much she loved her and didn't want her to leave and that she understood what she was talking about with her dad. She gave her commitment and word to do all she could to make it different. That she would go to the wall for her. Now, THAT was healing. The coded message was not.

When we speak in codes, our partner — and children — often don't realize that and take us quite literally. If your words are not accurate suddenly you have a problem that was so preventable, and you end up feeling misunderstood. Give them accurate words. Speak clearly, speak directly, and use words that are *true*.

I remember when I called my mother in the '80's to tell her I was thinking of leaving my hospital work and going into private practice full time. She exclaimed, "What?! Are you crazy? Why would you leave a paycheck — a sure thing — for a hope that you get clients? We're in a recession!" Fortunately, I knew enough to know she was speaking in code. Decoded: "I'm scared for you. I love you and want you to be safe."

Decoded messages are more vulnerable. You can do it. Stretch that comfort zone by deciding to let go of speaking in codes. This will increase the safety in your relationship.

One last word about codes, however. If in your family of origin your parents spoke in codes, it's a habit you've got. It may be the only way you have ever even seen communication. Be gentle with yourself. You simply must begin to examine the things you are saying and ask yourself if they are even true. Slow things down and *look for codes*. When you find one, like "Nothing," decode it. Figure out what message you really want to send and send that. Like practicing the piano, you will get better and better at decoding the more you do it.

Safety Review

Let's review the tools that are needed for making your relationship safe enough for your husband's emotional availability to develop.

1. Mutuality — you must be willing to be more vulnerable if you are asking him to be.

2. Create emotional safety by eliminating ALL physical abuse.

3. Create emotional safety by getting sober from alcohol and other chemicals.

4. Realize that raging is chemically addictive and, again, get sober. You MUST stop raging at your partner if you want him to be emotionally available to you. You've got to get this point.

5. Giving up control. This means giving up hurricaning in any form and being willing to stretch outside of your comfort zone. Be willing to free-fall.

6. Speak with a loving, kind voice, and practice being gentle. Drop the sarcasm, poisonous darts, attitude.

7. Have appropriate boundaries. Respond rather than react.

8. Be willing to say the hard stuff out loud.

9. Be in personal integrity, tell the truth. ALWAYS. Mark Twain used to say, "Always do right. This will gratify some people, and astonish the rest."

10. Decode your words.

Chapter 5

Resistances

Change is probably the most feared word in the English language. Somewhere deep in our psyche most of us have the concept of safety linked with the concept of keeping things the same. So, we resist change, we fight change, we hate change, we want change, but we wrestle change, we run from change, all the while we long for change, and yet some days, we are paralyzed by even the mere thought of it. Let's face it. We have a love/hate relationship with change. Mostly hate. And yet it is the ONLY thing in life, besides death, we can 100 percent count on happening.

I know you want change in your relationship or you wouldn't be reading this book. But I also know you have that part of your psyche that screams, "NO!" to change. Because even if the situation is bad that we're in, it has a certain comfortableness, because it's predictable and we know what to expect. The unknown is scary. What if it's worse than what we've got? Change often requires stepping into the unknown, into brand new territory. Risking making a fool out of ourselves. And so, even though our highest truth is that we want things to change — get better — we resist.

One of my friends, 15 years my junior, is a computer whiz. I, on the other hand, am a novice, to put it politely. Every time she wants me to learn a new capability on my computer, I kick and scream. She sends me links, and I yell, "Foul! Just put the information in an e-mail! Don't make me link anywhere!" She sends me attachments. "I don't know how to download attachments! And when I do manage to down-

load them (by simply clicking on the download button, mind you), I don't know how to locate them!" And, oh my, one time she asked me to put something on a spreadsheet for her! I just dug my heels in and said, "I can't. I don't know how to do that and I don't want to learn." She is patient with me; she is kind. She also refers to me as her friend whom she is dragging into the 21st century kicking and screaming the whole way.

That is resistance. Even though I know, theoretically, that my computer can do a gazillion things, some of which will make my life easier, I resist. Why? First of all, it's an unknown entity to me which brings up fear. Secondly, I feel stupid not knowing how to work this contraption that lives in my house. I know it's much smarter than I am, and I feel any new encounter I have with it, it will win. I'll be in the less than role scrambling, and it will be in the greater than role staring at me smugly. So I figure, why compete with a THING that's going to win every time anyway? Where's the fun in that?

My point is, resistance isn't necessarily rational. Rationally I know my computer isn't competing with me. Rationally I know I'm not stupid and I have all kinds of evidence that points to the exact opposite. Yet emotionally, it's a struggle to keep engaged in the process of growth and change when it comes to my computer. All the more so when it comes to our relationships.

Wrestling

Please note, resistance to change, especially change *you want to happen*, is an internal process. It is a fight you have with yourself. It is an emotional wrestling match with YOURSELF. In a way, that's the good news, because you're in charge of yourself. You can stop the resistance by actively talking through your fears in your head. You don't need anyone else's cooperation or permission. Simply by changing your self-talk you can reduce your resistance.

A good image for this is the mother in us taking care of the child in us. What would you say to a little child who is scared to try something

new? "It's okay. I'm going to help you. You can do it. I'm right here. Go on. Take your time. You're doing great. That's it. Good job!" These are things you have to learn to say to yourself when your resistance to change starts fighting you. Wake up your nurturing, rational self and put her in charge of your self-talk. Other helpful interventions include: You are not going to die. Trust the universe (or God). You're feeling scared which is normal for anyone when they try to change. Remember your highest truth: you want things to be better and in order for that to happen, you just have to walk through this scary part. You can do this. Don't make it bigger than it is. Breathe.

Erica Jong said, "If you risk nothing you risk even more." You can take care of yourself. Remember, too, Helen Reddy: "I am woman. I am strong." You are capable. You are competent.

Mentors

Also, there might be people who have inspired you whom you can think of, and draw strength and determination from. Or calmness. For example, in my life when I face my own resistance to a change I'm choosing, a change I *want*, I think of my mother. My mother left my alcoholic, sociopathic, unfaithful father when I was 3. She left with 2 babies, no money, and no education beyond high school. She was 26. She said to herself over, and over, and over again, "I will not raise my children in this," as she daily marched one foot in front of the other walking through her fears. So, when I need strength, I think of her. I think, "If she could do THAT and survive, I can do THIS."

Recognizing Resistances

I'm going to outline some common resistances I see, but there are probably as many unique resistances as there are people. You will have to figure out your own games that you play with yourself when you are in resistance.

I Can Do It Better — With one couple I met, the wife lamented that her husband did not help enough with the baby. It was their first child and she was overwhelmed with all the feedings, baths, clothes changes, diaper changes, bottle washings, rocking, laundry, etc. She desperately wanted more help from her partner. When I listened to her story, it did seem she was doing way more than her part, and it made sense why she wanted things to change. Furthermore, her husband wholeheartedly agreed that it needed to change and seemed not only willing to help more, but anxious to. The problem? Resistance. It seems that time after time when the husband provided more help, the wife monitored him and told him he was doing it wrong. In feeding, he wasn't holding the baby right. In dressing, he was choosing the "wrong" outfit for the weather. In diaper changing, he forgot the baby powder. Sometimes she'd go so far as to say, "Here, let me do it," and take the baby away from him! The consequence? She was getting more and more adept at handling the baby while he was getting more and more insecure about his abilities. This is resistance. The wife was actually encouraging the system to develop in exactly the way she was saying didn't work for her. She didn't have room for her husband's learning curve.

If you want change from your husband, you have to have room for his learning curve. Change takes time and practice. Don't short-circuit the change you long for by expecting it to be instantaneous. Be careful how much you criticize your partner when he's trying something new.

The Cold Shoulder — Depending on your husband's history, this resistance may or may not be in your relationship. One man I worked with whose mother slipped into depressions when he was a child and then refused to talk to anyone, would do ANYTHING when his wife would "freeze him out." The wife said she wanted her husband to be more present in the relationship and not such a pushover. And I believed her. I believed that was her highest truth and that in the depths of her soul, she really wanted that to happen. The problem? Resistance. Each time the husband tried even meekly to assert himself, she would "freeze him out." She would be cordial and polite to him, but offer no warmth, no support, no encouragement. She would say, "Fine,"

to his wanting to do something his way and then "punish" him with the cold shoulder for days. He had learned that the agony of the cold shoulder, being shut out, wasn't worth ANY self-definition he might risk. Again, the wife was actually encouraging the system to stay exactly the way she did not want it.

Never Enough — This resistance means your husband can't win. You are the bottomless pit that no matter what he does, it isn't enough. You ask for emotional availability and when he starts to open up, you minimize it. You raise the bar. A common phrase from your lips is, "Yes, but..." "Yes, you mowed the lawn, but you didn't edge. I thought you'd edge." One wife I worked with wanted more affection from her husband. She longed for non-sexual hugs, hand-holding, and spontaneous kisses that didn't necessarily lead to the bedroom. Her complaint was that the only time he touched her was "when he wanted to have sex." Her husband was willing to change. Then in comes resistance. As they were *leaving my office*, the husband reached over and gave his wife a kiss on the cheek to which she coolly replied, "One little kiss is not going to make up for 10 years of neglect." You see, he was dead in the water before he even got started swimming. The message was: no matter what you do it won't be enough. How encouraging is THAT?

Another way to look at this type of resistance is on a number scale. If your goal is #100 behavior from your partner (let's say, being comfortable being emotionally available to you), and he is only at behavior #10 (scared out of his wits but very committed to trying), this resistance will beat your husband up at every step from 10 to 100 because it's not 100 behavior. Number 11 isn't good enough, #12 isn't, of course #13 isn't, etc. The problem is, at some point, your husband will get so discouraged, he'll quit. And you'll never get to the #100 behavior *that you want*. Resistance.

Hurricaning/Raging — This resistance keeps you from being heard. I, like you probably, have a vivid picture in my head of people fleeing from the collapsed towers of the World Trade Center with a

huge ball of smoke and dust and debris in the background rapidly rolling towards them threatening to overtake the very air they had to breathe. Panic on their faces. Terror. I assure you if any of them had run into their partner standing there saying, "I want you to be more available to me," the words would not have even computed. Even remotely. They were, literally, running for their lives. This is *emotionally* what happens to your partner when you are hurricaning/raging at him. He begins to run for his life, and his listening capacity *shuts down*. He is in trauma. That is, by hurricaning/raging, you are actually PREVENTING change from happening. This is a very powerful resistance to change. You must call yourself on it. If you want change to happen — and I believe you do — hurricaning and raging won't get you there. Yes, your husband needs to hear the message you are sending. It is important and he needs to "get it." Yet you must take care that you are not preventing that from happening.

I remember one particular "discussion" I was having with my husband years ago where, in a calm voice, I was relentlessly hammering home my point. After ten or fifteen minutes of this I noticed he was staring off into space. Frustrated, I said, "Do you understand what I'm saying?" to which he replied, "No, I can't even hear you talking." My relentlessness had turned off his ability to hear. Resistance.

Denial — One resistance to change is making things really "not that bad" that really *are* that bad. This often happens when one partner has an addiction. I want him to be more emotionally available to me, but I also pretend with him that he is just a social drinker. Or that his going into the office on Sundays makes sense because he is so good at his job that nobody else can do any of his work as well as he can. We ignore the real problem of addiction and instead attack something tangential — which, of course, keeps change from happening.

It's a way to stay safe and within our comfort zone all the while pretending — to ourselves — we are working on change.

When I was a new therapist one of my first clients was a woman who came to me complaining of her work situation and wanting to change jobs. Then she was distraught over the lack of connection she

had with her husband. Could we do couple's therapy? She also talked of her lack of true friends, her bad relationship with her family of origin, her feelings of isolation, and her poor housekeeping skills. As I probed deeper, I asked about her drug and alcohol usage. She described herself as a "social drinker," who, when on the rare occasions she and her husband went out, would only have 1-2 drinks the whole evening. Furthermore, she never did drugs. Never had, never would. That seemed reasonable.

So we started to look at her issues one at a time. Week after week I kept feeling there was no deep level change happening and I wondered why. Then she called my office at midnight one night — drunk. Turns out she was a "social drinker" in public and a "closet drinker" at home. She drank a 12-pack of beer every night! Her denial system, and my lack of experience, let her "pretend" she was doing therapy and was sincerely working on change. Again, resistance.

In summary, change is so frightening to most of us that we inevitably develop resistances subconsciously. The only way to battle these, of course, is to bring them to your conscious level. Become aware of them. Know your games. Look for them.

Chapter 6

Learning to Love/Learning to Heal

It seems that the essence of all the great religions of the world — Christianity, Judaism, Islam, Buddhism, etc. — can be boiled down inevitably to one word: love. Now, I am not so delusional to think I can write a lesson on love more effectively than the *Bible*, the *Koran*, the *Torah*, or the *I Ching*. These are great texts and deserve great study. Here, I only offer humbly meager thoughts on the subject, perhaps with a word or two that will click for you.

The topic of love is immense. It is a lifetime project. It is something we must consciously work at daily. Loving reminds me of children's stories that are written on many levels. "Gulliver's Travels" for example is a delightful story of a giant landing among a world of thousands of tiny people who "capture" him. To a child it is a fun and exciting story. But it's also the story of the tyranny of the British monarchy in a class system where the lower class had no rights. To an adult it is a daring and satirical story full of oppression and ultimately liberation. Which description of the story is true? Both. So it is with love.

Love is a concept that exists on many levels. It seems the older and wiser a person gets, the more levels they can see. There is the surface, lustful "feeling" level of love which, of course, is wonderful. There is the love that we feel for our children. This is probably as close to unconditional love we, as humans, can express and experience. It's a love so deep that we become willing to sacrifice even our very lives to save them. What mother watching her 10-year-old child dying of cancer wouldn't take on the disease herself if it would heal

her child? Then there is a love that let's us love the unlovable. It's the love that let's us respond kindly even to strangers whose behaviors are rude and "undeserving." To say a kind word, "You must be having a hard day. I hope it gets better." To extend a hand, "Can I help somehow?" It's the love that lets us offer a smile or a hug: even to a porcupine.

There's a love that allows us to forgive, to let go of, to go forward. It takes this love to be able to say, "I know what you did was really hurtful to me, but I've done hurtful things in my lifetime, too. I understand, and I'm choosing to put that behind us and to forgive you." There's a love that lets us overlook others' imperfections. There's a love that helps us be proactive: to plan surprises, to anticipate need, to take action when someone is hurting. There's self-love: where we are kind to ourselves, say nice things to ourselves, and have good boundaries. There's even a love that can pull us out of despair, pick up the pieces, and help us start over again. This love can be found in a child's innocence, in nature, in God. And then, last, but not least, there is what I call conscious choice love.

Conscious Choice Love

Conscious choice love is an active, conscious **decision** to care for someone. To look out for them, to encourage and preserve what is important to them, to help them, to heal them. Here love is an action verb. It's not so much a "feeling" as a "doing." Doing things on purpose to care for another person. In the context of this book that other person would be your partner. It's a decision to think about that other person on purpose and to actively DO something that would care for him. If you've been disconnected from love for a while because your partner hasn't been meeting your needs, the most important step to reconnection is a DECISION to love again. Without this conscious choice on your part, it is unlikely your system can heal.

Now, I'm clear down in Texas and I can already hear you screaming, "What about HIM? Why do *I* have to be the one to consciously

choose love?" The answer is three fold. First, because if you don't, your relationship will, most likely, not change. Second, because love is healing whether you give or receive it, and you need healing. And third, your partner has to consciously choose it, too. The goal is win/win where he wins AND you win.

Behavior On Purpose

So, *if* you decide to consciously choose to care for your partner again, to love him on purpose, that is, it must be translated into BE-HAVIOR. I suggest that you do one behavior per day. Just one on purpose behavior where you do something to care for your partner. It could be big or it could be small. Maybe you call him and say I hope you're having a good day. Or you do a load of his laundry. Or you surprise him for lunch. Or you turn back the sheets on his side of the bed for him. Or you buy him tickets to the basketball game. Or you decide not to criticize him all day. It doesn't matter what it is as long as it is a conscious, on purpose action on your part to take care of him. This must become a habit where your goal is to consciously choose love daily and to do loving behaviors. The long term goal is to learn to care for your husband's hopes and dreams as much as you care for your own. The bottom line is you must do your part to change the system. It will not get better without your active, loving participation. If you want to be loved, you must love.

Conditional Love

I am, however, not talking about loving unconditionally. I believe love in a marriage needs to be conditional. To love your partner unconditionally is to have no boundaries. To love unconditionally means I will love you no matter what you do or say. This we can offer to our children, but not our partners. That's because marriage is a RECIP-ROCAL relationship. With our children, it is *our* job to meet *their*

emotional needs. It is not their job to meet ours. With our partner, it is our job to meet his needs AND his job to meet ours. Therefore, the condition of love in marriage is that it will be reciprocal. The "condition" that has to exist in order for love to flourish is one of mutuality, reciprocity. I am not saying love your husband even if your needs never get met. Yuck. Who would want that kind of marriage? I am saying love your husband and have the expectation of love being returned to you. I am also saying do not expect your husband to love you unconditionally. He needs reciprocity and mutuality, too.

There is one more "condition," that also must be met before people are able to consistently consciously choose to love. That condition? Safety. Emotional and physical safety. That is, I will love you — take care of you on purpose — if you will create safety for me. That usually means being faithful and honest. It also means no physical abuse or even the threat of that. It sometimes means being realistic about money. It sometimes means get sober.

So really, I am asking you to: first, consciously **decide** to actively love your partner. That is, check back into your relationship. And second, set forth two conditions that must be met by him:

#1 reciprocity and #2 safety.

I am also asking you to provide those two conditions TO your husband. You must love in order to be loved.

Postscript: If you feel you love your husband unconditionally and that you really will continue to love him no matter what he says or does, then your conditions need to be about staying with him. Sometimes a woman must leave a relationship even when her heart is still filled with love for her partner. I see this in battering relationships. I hear from my clients who have a black eye or three broken ribs, "I can't leave him. I still love him." Fine. Still love him. But come to know that you will only STAY with him if the conditions of reciprocity and safety are met. This requires listening to your brain as well as your heart. Sometimes it means letting your brain overrule your heart. You deserve reciprocity and safety in your primary relationship. Make

those the conditions that must be met in order for you to stay. If these conditions are not met, let your brain take over, pack your things, and move on. This, I promise you, you will not regret long term. Short term, yes; every minute. Long term, *never*.

Ten Points to Ponder About Safety

Some of this is review but worth looking at again.

1. You cannot create safety if you are a bottomless pit and take up all the space. "Me, me, me, meet MY needs," lets you know you are off track. Only in getting out of yourself will you be able to see his woundedness. Remember, his wound is 10 percent now, 90 percent history and so IT IS NOT ABOUT YOU (even if he tells you it is).

2. Consciously choose to hear what your partner is saying rather than rebutting it. He has important information to give you.

3. You cannot create safety if you are hurricaning and/or raging at your partner. Physical abuse, as well, is a destructive force, and eliminates the possibility of safety.

4. Get aware of the criticism that pours forth from your mouth. People THRIVE on positive reinforcement. They wither with criticism. I asked a client of mine to commit to saying ONE positive about her husband to her husband that day. She was so furious about not getting her emotional needs met for so long that she couldn't think of ANY comment that was positive. I kept pushing and she finally committed to coming up with one after leaving my office. Her positive? "That green shirt looks nice on you." The result? Her husband wore that green shirt 3 times — even washed it himself — that week. THAT is the power of positives.

5. Adjust your tone of voice. Screaming "I love you" with an angry, hateful tone doesn't feel like love to the receiver. It

feels confusing and dishonest. Consciously choosing to love means consciously choosing to speak in a loving voice so the love comes across. Otherwise, you're not really LOVING — you're just pretending.

6. Be honest and tell the truth.

7. Be faithful — both emotionally and physically.

8. Get sober.

9. Be in personal integrity.

10. Have appropriate boundaries.

Chapter 7

Exceptions: When Your Partner Will Never Be Emotionally Available

Most people are capable of emotional availability. However, there is a small percentage of people who were so damaged emotionally at a very young age that they will never — at least not in this lifetime — be capable of being emotionally available to you or to anyone. These people were what we call unbonded children.

Unbonded children, children with a severe attachment disorder, are children who did not attach or emotionally bond to a primary caretaker between the ages of 0 and 2. It was not their fault. Their caretakers were not able to be consistent enough for bonding to occur for a variety of reasons. Maybe because of their own emotional traumas or holes from their own childhoods. Maybe their business deteriorated rapidly then failed and financial devastation ensued. Maybe another child had a terminal illness and died, or a child died unexpectedly. Maybe their partner beat them or walked out on them and left for another woman. Maybe they were overwhelmed with too many children and not enough help. Maybe the child was taken from the home and lived in several foster homes. There are lots of reasons, but the bottom line is the child did not get the bonding necessary in order to feel emotionally safe at the core of his soul.

Most research shows that if we don't get through to this child and have him bond with someone by the age of 8, then we lose him. That is, he so thoroughly cuts off from his own emotions in order to survive and buries them so deeply that they are not retrievable. Occasionally a child is able to bond as late as age ten, eleven or

even twelve ,* but it is a rare and very difficult task. Usually by age 8, when there is a major developmental shift in the brain, the child has learned not to trust anyone and that the world is not safe.

Lack of Empathy

The biggest damage is the child's loss of an ability to develop empathy. Empathy is being able to feel what another person feels. It helps us not hurt other people because we relate to their pain. That is, it causes us pain to watch another person suffer. For example, we don't steal from people because we know how badly it feels to be stolen from. Unbonded children lack this empathy, and they grow into unbonded adults who cannot be taught empathy. They don't "get" the other person's emotional experience.

Unbonded children/adults also lack remorse. They are not sorry when they hurt someone. In fact, it may give them a sense of power and justice to do so. These are children who grow up to be able to commit crimes and not lose any sleep over them. These are our most damaged children: the ones who lack an emotional connection with themselves, and therefore with others. These are our society's sociopaths.

I worked for one year in a maximum security prison for children. The population was male, ages 15–21, 87 percent homicides and rapists. If a child committed multiple murders he could be sent to our facility as young as 13. There I was taught the triage model that was developed on the battlefields of World War II. Originally this was used to assess medical need. Doctors going onto the battlefields had to put each wounded man into one of three categories. The first category was: no matter how much time, attention, and intervention I give this man, he will still die. The second category was: no matter how little

---

* "The Twelfth Door," *Reader's Digest*, December, 1997, pp. 116–121, pp. 193–226; excerpt from book, *The Things I Want Most*, by Richard F. Miniter.

time, attention, and intervention I give this man, he will still live. The third category was the soldier that the doctor treated: if he gets my time, attention and intervention he will live; if he does not get it, he will die.

So it was in the prison. We were asked to assess, basically, who was sociopathic and who was not. Then of those who were not, who were fully connected to empathy and remorse, and who were bonded just enough that intense intervention could help them onto a path of rehabilitation and redirection. Those in the last category were the boys who got most of the staff's time, attention, and intervention. The sociopaths, the boys who had committed multiple murders, bragged about them with no remorse and no empathy, and who, if released promised to kill further, tragically, were beyond rehabilitation. Their emotional damage, again so tragically, had been too severe for them to ever be able to develop empathy. These are the Charles Mansons, the Ted Bundys.

Sociopaths in Relationships

So, what does this have to do with relationships? It is my belief that we have more sociopaths, unbonded children, in our society than first meets the eye. There seems to be a subcategory of sociopaths who don't use violence at all. They would never physically harm someone directly — though they may hire someone to do so — because the consequences *to themselves* would be too high a price to pay. The consequences not being guilt and remorse and emotional suffering, but having their freedoms taken away from them. They, therefore, wouldn't risk such behavior. They are, however, able to climb up the ladder at work by stepping on other people's heads all the way to the top without blinking an eye.

They are experts at playing two roles: they very much see themselves as the hero and yet all the while see themselves as the victim. It's the wife beater who beats her behind closed doors because she treats him so badly. No remorse, no shame, instead somehow vindi-

cated. It's the boss who is able to negotiate his employees' contracts down to almost nothing while collecting his own two million dollar salary.

Another characteristic of sociopathology is the sociopath's ability to be charming. In fact, "charming" is the adjective I most hear when a person is describing someone in her life that might be sociopathic. "He can charm anyone" is a red flag. Because of course he can. Since he has no connections to a conscience he can say anything to anyone, whether it's true or not, without even a twinge of guilt or feeling bad.

How do you recognize if you are with a sociopath? It is very difficult because we all do crummy things sometimes. None among us is not capable of very hurtful, even hateful behaviors. But with a sociopath, there is a PATTERN of such behavior with a PATTERN of no remorse. It is not a one time event. It is how a person lives his life. Characteristics to look for:

1. He's charming.

2. He sees himself as a hero and a victim.

3. He seems to have no connection to a conscience — he can emotionally hurt other people and it doesn't seem to bother him.

4. He may say "I'm sorry" easily, glibly, but he doesn't seem to actually feel remorse.

5. He doesn't demonstrate empathy; he doesn't seem to relate to "the other" experience.

Examples

A personal example that crystallized my father's sociopathology for me happened one Christmas several years ago. My oldest was about 5 when my father called to tell me he had bought my son a Nintendo 64 for the holiday. This new toy had just come out and was hard to get, but he had managed to buy one. I took a deep breath and said I was

sorry he hadn't called me to talk about it first, since my husband and I had already decided we didn't want him to have a Nintendo 64 that Christmas. I explained to him that because we already had a Super Nintendo and we didn't want to encourage consumerism in our children — having to run out and buy the newest, latest and greatest version of whatever was on the market — that we were planning to skip the Nintendo 64 craze. Our conversation follows:

Dad   My grandson wants a Nintendo 64, he'll get a Nintendo 64, and he'll get it from ME.

Patti   But, Dad, do you understand we don't want him to have one and that we will not let him keep it?

Dad   On Christmas morning I'm showing up with a Nintendo 64 for my grandson.

Patti   Do you understand that will cause him pain? That you will give it to him and we will not let him keep it? Do you understand he will hurt if you do what you plan to do?

Dad   Yeah, but *I'll* be the hero — *you'll* be the villain. (And he roared with laughter.)

You see, his giving wasn't about taking care of my son — it was okay to cause him pain. It was, however, about my dad looking like the good guy. He could feel great about himself being such a hero *even though* his behavior would cause pain to a 5-year-old little boy. This is sociopathology. It cannot be cured. It cannot be healed. It cannot be reasoned with — because there is no connection to a conscience.

Another example of sociopathology is from Joseph Wambaugh's nonfiction book, *The Onion Field*. Here the prosecutor sits with the defendant, questioning him about the children left behind after he murdered their father, Ian Campbell.

One day Byrne asked the defendant, "How do you *really* feel about those kids, Greg?"

"What kids?" asked Greg.

"Campbell's kids," said Byrne. "And about Campbell?"

"To tell you the honest truth, Mr. Byrne, I feel nothing."

"Nothing?"

"Nothing about them. Any of them. But I *will* send them money if I ever make any. Because I said I would."

There it was, Byrne thought. The sociopathic personality. Greg looked at the tall prosecutor apologetically. "It was as though he *wished* he could say he felt something about the murder," Byrne explained. "Wishing he could feel something, because he knew other people did. It was the first time I ever truly understood sociopathy. It just wasn't there. He just had no remorse in his makeup."

He knows — intellectually — that he SHOULD feel something for the victim's family, but he doesn't. Again, this is behavior beyond recovery.

If you are living with or married to such a man, he will not be able to be emotionally available to you — ever. He can be charming and make you feel like he's there for you, but in the next beat rip you to shreds without it disturbing his morning coffee or reading of the paper. I find that women involved with sociopaths spend much of their time and energy and LIVES trying to get their partner to "get it." Sadly, they can't get it. Long before they met you the deep emotional damage was done. Some things do not heal. This is one of them. I know that's so counter to our American never-say-die attitude. It's so against our very fiber that says we can do anything, fix anything, work harder and come up with a solution. I'm sorry. Some things do not heal. This is one of them.

Tough Cases

Besides sociopathology I believe everything else is healable, at least to a degree. That is, all the other emotional damage and trauma

we have as a child can be, to a certain extent, reversed. In some cases, unlocked. And yet life is finite. We only have so many years. Sometimes the emotional work your partner needs to do may take too long for you. Sometimes the amount of effort it would take on your part is more than you want to invest. So, just because it may be healable to a certain extent doesn't necessarily mean your needs will get met in a timely manner or even enough. Let's look at some tough cases.

Addiction — Someone who has an addiction has their primary relationship with their substance or addictive behavior. Not you. Are you ever going to get your emotional needs met in this relationship on a long-term, consistent basis? No.

Not as long as the addiction is present. You must be willing to confront your partner's problem directly and give him a time frame (I usually recommend up to a month) to get into treatment. Tell him you will not be able to stay with him long term if he is not willing to get sober. Then give yourself six months of observation. This means just quietly observing. Do not nag him about treatment or his addiction. Do not gently remind him. Do not tell him you are in a six month observation period. You will be tempted to push him to get into treatment during this time period because you REALLY want to stay with him and that means he REALLY has to get it. But don't do it. Observe quietly. Be a detective and silently gather information. If he doesn't get into treatment within the month and his addiction has continued for your six months of observation, HE is not serious about getting sober. YOU may be serious about his getting sober, but HE is not. He will not get sober based on your being serious about it. If six months pass without any action on his part, he is not going to get sober — no matter what he tells you. Listen to the behavior and not the words. To stay with him beyond the six months you will be investing way too much of your life for way too little return. You deserve to be with someone who will have their primary relationship with YOU and not with an addiction.

Mental Illness — This covers a broad spectrum of illnesses including major depression, bipolar disorder (formerly known as manic-depression), schizophrenia, obsessive compulsive disorder (OCD), borderline personality disorder, and debilitating anxiety disorders. My belief is that for most people these disorders are treatable and manageable. They are most effectively treated with medication as well as psychotherapy. These disorders are often not "cured," but managed. If they are cured, they often — but not always — take a long time to heal. Years.

I do believe people with these illnesses can learn to be emotionally available to you. The question becomes, do they want to address the problems? Are they willing to do what it takes to be in charge of the illness instead of it being in charge of them? One woman I worked with married a man who was bipolar. She knew he was bipolar before they married. He knew he was bipolar. He took medication and worked with a therapist regularly. He was a delightful man and was able to keep his extreme swings in balance.

However, after they married he decided — on his own — that he wasn't bipolar anymore. He stopped taking his medication and seeing his therapist. A $15,000 credit card shopping spree followed. When his wife found out about this she was, understandably, very upset. This threw him into a depressive state where he refused to get out of bed and spent hours crying. She took him back to the psychiatrist where he again began medication and therapy. By the time I met her she had been married to this man 10 years and had been through this cycle four times. The fifth time her husband declared himself "cured," she left him. Because life is finite, she decided ten years was enough of a chance for her husband to get in charge of his illness. It didn't have to go away for her to stay, but it did have to be consistently managed, which her husband was not able and/or willing to do.

If your partner has a mental illness, is he fighting it? Is he winning? I'm not suggesting that if your husband has a major depressive episode that you should leave him. "Is it a pattern, and is he doing something about it?" becomes the question. Are you able to sustain hope that progress is happening?

Power People — I talked about this some on the men's side of the book. I think it's important on this side of the book to examine whether or not the person you are with is a power person. Certainly sociopaths are power people. They cannot conceive of a win/win situation because they don't have empathy to even consider the other person's needs. But not all power people are sociopaths. In fact I've met some very nice power people. Kind, good-hearted, but nonetheless power people. Unlike sociopaths, these power people seem to be ruled by fear. Almost a terror. Often these people are so utterly controlling because they fear things ever getting out of control. Or they don't feel internally in control, so they try to control all the externals.

I find this particularly true with people whose childhoods were marked with extreme chaos and/or constant change. They grew up in an environment that was so unsafe emotionally that it put them into a sort of perpetual terror. This could be from something so obvious as being raised with an out of control raging alcoholic parent to something seemingly benign like the father got transferred often and the child had to move eight times in ten years. I worked with one man who went to twelve elementary schools (that he could remember). It is no small wonder then that these people grow up to be very controlling, at some level trying to prevent what happened to them as a child from *ever* happening again. Depending on the amount of trauma these people carry, they may or may not be able to be there for you emotionally. They may really want to be, but are simply too afraid that they might again fall into that black hole of terror they experienced as a child. It's, at some level, a form of post traumatic stress disorder. In order to stay with such a power person, you would need to be able to recognize his extreme fear and insecurity plus see significant effort and progress on his part in changing it.

Please know, however, power people can usually get *better*, but it is rare for them to completely stop their automatic tendency toward control. Often they come from homes where one parent was a power person. They have seen role-modeled daily that this is *how to be* in the world. You are asking them to restructure themselves at a core level. Yes, it can be done, but I feel psychotherapy or some kind of intervention is imperative.

Psychotherapy can help the power person identify and understand the almost panic that begins to swallow him up if he doesn't get to dictate everything. A mixed group therapy (of men and women) is often very helpful. Again, in my opinion, if a power person does not address the root cause behind his "control freak" behavior, he will not be able to change it and therefore will not be able to be there for you emotionally. He's too scared at a core level, though he may be completely unaware of this. Power people cannot compute the concept of win/win. They equate your winning with their losing which means that security base is yanked from under them again. They develop a "take no prisoners" attitude. Winning provides emotional safety to them, and they will go to any length to get that safety.

In other words, this is not an easy issue to resolve. Genuine connection with another person involves risking emotionally which feels a little out of control for all of us. For the power person, he CANNOT allow himself to feel that because it triggers him back to that black hole where life was not safe.

I believe this can be overcome — I've seen it done — but not without great effort and commitment.

Battering — What if your husband hits you in a fit of rage? This is absolutely a primitive way of responding on your husband's part. And it's not okay. Ever. You must have a very clear boundary about this. Clear in yourself and clear to your partner. Yes, you may have said things that were inciting, insulting, rude, and way out of line, but that does not give *anyone* the right to hit you. Ever. I would say you must stop verbally abusing your husband because he needs to be healed by you, and you can't heal him if you're verbally battering him. I would say to your husband DO NOT allow yourself to be verbally battered. Have a boundary. Say out loud, "I will not be talked to that way. You are verbally abusing me, and I will no longer be verbally abused. I need you to change the way you are talking to me." I would tell your husband to leave YOU if you were not willing or able to change your pattern. But never, NEVER, ever to hit. Your partner must develop an internal boundary that says, "I will NEVER hit my partner again."

You must help him do this by having a ZERO tolerance for physical violence toward you.

You must clearly state in a moment of calmness, "If you hit me again, I will not be in your life. I promise you to work on my verbal battering of you, but regardless of how I do on that, you may not hit me again. If you walk out because I'm being verbally abusive, I understand. I support you in doing that. That will help me stop MY pattern. But you must NEVER hit me again, or I will not be with you. Do you understand?"

Then, if it happens again, you MUST leave. Why? Because a PATTERN of battering is established after the second incident. It will become your life. Do you want this for your life? You will not get your emotional needs met consistently and long term in this pattern. By staying you are saying to your partner, "I give you permission to hit me again." I don't want to insult your intelligence by stating the obvious, but this is not good for you. Or him. You deserve to be loved and cared for.

Love and caring does not include hitting. If you want to be loved — not just have the words said to you, but actually LOVED — then you must leave anyone who hits you. You are not a child. You are not a victim. Pack your bags, take your kids, call the women's center in your area or 911 to ask for help, and don't look back. That's the most important part: don't look back. You can end the battering cycle by being the one who says, "No more." Look forward. You can do it. And you must do it: for your sake and for your children's.

Surprise Tough Cases

There are two tough cases that, on the surface, don't look like tough cases. They look benign. Yet if your partner struggles with either of these, emotional availability will not come easily for him. They are ADD/ADHD and a history of emotional incest.

ADD/ADHD — Here I'll use one symbol, ADD, to represent both

ADD (attention deficit disorder) and ADHD (attention deficit disorder with hyperactivity) because both feel similar as far as emotional availability to the partner is concerned. ADD is not a mental illness. Research suggests that ADD is a physical condition where the frontal lobe of the brain does not receive as many electrical impulses as do the brains of people who do not have ADD. This frontal lobe of our brain is rather like our CEO. It's the part that organizes and shouts out orders and plans to the rest of the brain. It lets us plan ahead, focus and get things done, remember commitments, organize and prioritize, and assess situations quickly on a multifaceted level. People with ADD have a deficit of electrical impulses in this area. They don't have a deficit of impulses in other areas of the brain — in fact, they have an *abundance* of impulses — but they do have a deficit in the area that can organize, prioritize, and filter out those other impulses.

Since only about 5–7 percent of our population have this deficit, 93–95 percent of our population do not. This means we do not live in an ADD world. Our world is not designed for people with ADD which makes it extra hard for them to be effective here. Instead, it's designed for people who are able to plan ahead, be organized, get things done, remember commitments, etc. Therefore, I think of ADD as a handicap — at least in our society.

Life for a person with ADD has an extra layer of struggle because what comes naturally and so easily for almost everyone they meet, comes only with Herculean effort to them, if at all. It's a little bit like dyslexia. Our society is designed for people who can read and write. If a person can't read and write easily, it's a handicap they deal with daily — at least in our society. Perhaps in society of 2000 years ago, where literacy was limited to the priests and aristocracy, dyslexia wasn't a handicap at all. But today it is. So it is with ADD. Maybe in society even 200 years ago when life wasn't as complex technologically and was lived at a slower pace, ADD may not have even been noticed. There was time for daydreaming. Today, in our go-go-go society, there isn't.

What does this have to do with emotional availability? First of all, a person with ADD is often using so much time and so much energy

just trying to survive in this — what seems to them — overwhelming world, that it's hard for them to have time and energy left for emotional availability. I worked with a client from western war-ravaged Russia who spent his childhood years in survival mode: fighting for his life, stealing food, hiding from the rebels. It wasn't until his 20's, when he was able to emigrate to the U.S., that he even had the *experience* of introspection. He didn't even know that existed when he lived in Russia. It is a similar experience for people with ADD, particularly undiagnosed and untreated ADD. They have little time for depth and introspection because they are so overwhelmed with *life*. Just trying to survive.

Social Deficit. For people with ADD, it's as if they have twelve radio stations playing in their heads at once. It is difficult for them not to skip from one station to another. This often makes conversation disjointed. This is why the person with ADD can, in the middle of what you consider to be a deep conversation, say something like, "I forgot to tell you but I heard on the radio it's supposed to rain tomorrow." This can be maddening to the partner who does not have ADD. It can feel invalidating, even crazy-making, if you don't understand how your partner's brain works and that it's not about you. It can be embarrassing in social situations when your partner says a non sequitur that doesn't seem to connect to the conversation at all. It can feel hopeless when your partner forgets — again — to write down his ATM withdrawals in the checkbook. It can feel exhausting.

There Is Hope. The hope is in diagnosis and treatment. If your partner is disorganized, surrounded by piles of clutter, unable to focus, unable to finish things, seems "spaced out" at times, takes two hours to do something you could do in thirty minutes, or talks fast and nonstop and can't seem to sit still for a moment, he may have ADD or ADHD. It's imperative he be diagnosed and treated as well as educated about it.

So often I meet couples where ADD is prominent in their relationship, wrecking havoc, and it hasn't even been identified. They are therefore fighting in the dark. They are attacking the wrong problem. They are trying to address each of the one million trees instead of

seeing the forest. ADD is the forest. It manifests itself a million different ways, but it must be dealt with on the forest level. Diagnosis allows you to start addressing the *problem* and not the many *symptoms*. Like dyslexia, if this disorder is not recognized in a child and properly treated, he will continue to fail in a system designed for non-dyslexics. If, however, the child is diagnosed, he can be taught to read using an appropriate tool: a reading program designed for dyslexics. He can also skip years of frustration and low self-esteem. So it is with ADD. Diagnosis is CRITICAL.

Understanding of the disorder is essential if you are going to love this man and if he is going to meet your emotional needs. I recommend reading Dr. Edward Hallowell and Dr. John Ratey's book, *Driven to Distraction*, ten times. Men with ADD are capable of emotional availability but most readily with diagnosis, treatment (which may include medication to stimulate the frontal lobe of the brain), and education. Like blindness, ADD does not go away, but must be managed throughout life. And, like blindness, ADD, though a handicap, can be managed so well that the person with ADD can lead a fully functioning life. The key is in taking action and addressing the problem.

Postscript: For whatever reason people with handicaps seem to have their own areas of giftedness. Someone who is blind often "sees" better than those of us with two perfectly functioning eyes. A Downs Syndrome child is refreshingly able to express love so profoundly. Beethoven was deaf when he wrote some of his best music. So it is with ADD.

Most people with ADD are very bright and very creative. They are able to skip steps we linear thinkers are not. They are able to envision possibilities differently than those without ADD. A lot of clinicians believe Ben Franklin probably had ADHD and that Thomas Edison did as well. Many of the world's great artists and actors, inventors and scientists have had ADD or ADHD. Yes, in our society it is a handicap, but yes, it is a giftedness, too. In order for your partner to be emotionally available to you, you and he must understand this.

Emotional Incest — If you are married to someone who was the chosen child, the hero child, or the surrogate spouse, you're in for a

tough go. An over-bonded parent-child relationship teaches the child that loving someone or being loved by someone means disappearing. Even connecting at all to someone means disappearing. Emotional intimacy definitely does. Men who were emotionally incested as children report feeling "controlled" by their partner and that they have no choices. They have little or no boundaries because, as a child they weren't allowed to have boundaries. Emotional incest destroys the lines that differentiate the child from the parent. That is, the parent invades the child's personal emotional space. The child is asked to take care of the parent emotionally even if it means selling his soul. Here are a few case studies from my practice. Details and names have been changed to protect anonymity.

The important thing to realize as you read these case studies is: I am only one therapist. I can name one hundred people I've worked with over the years who were emotionally incested as children. Then think of all the therapists there are and all their case studies. Then think of all the men who have never gone to a therapist and so aren't even represented in the statistics. My point is, emotional incest is more common than we think. It may be in your relationship and worth looking for.

Jim's mother had always been considerably overweight and took him on eating sprees as far back as he could remember. They ate together and got fat together. The boy got teased unmercifully at school for his weight to which his mother responded by reinforcing their "special bond": she was the only one who understood. To ease his pain she cooked him some of his favorite comfort foods for dinner. Then in junior high he decided to lose weight. He says, "I remember her screaming at me to eat the homemade cookies she had just pulled out of the oven." She was very angry and upset with him for breaking their secret unspoken pact where only they would love each other — and insisted he eat with her. I asked what he did. "I ate the cookies." As a child he could not risk upsetting his mother that much, possibly losing her.

Tom's parents divorced when he was 8. His father made Tom his best friend. They boated together, rode motorcycles together, went on vacations together, explored new restaurants, built projects, shared dreams, etc. The boy became what the father "lived for." When my client became a teenager he, naturally, wanted to go out and do things with his school friends. His father raged at him to stop being so irresponsible and to work on the remodeling project they had both committed to. Then he played the martyr role and "guilted" him about even asking. "I felt like a prisoner. I spent the whole summer with my *Dad* rebuilding his house."

John described being raised with an alcoholic mother. His father traveled a lot and he was the oldest son. "I'd get my brother and sister up and ready for school, then I'd fix my mom's coffee and take it to her. I used to get so mad and tell her she needed to be a MOTHER and take care of us. She'd just cry and say how sorry she was, and that just made me feel worse."

Dallas was an only child who lived with his divorced father. He was his father's chosen whipping post. No matter what Dallas did, his father's way was better. He remembers mowing the lawn and as soon as he finished, his father doing it again. Dallas has spent a lifetime trying to make his father happy and get his approval.

David watched his father rage at his older brother. He became a quiet child much to his father's liking. He also spent hours doing still life paintings his father set up for him. He didn't particularly like painting, but his father had always wished that he could leave his job and become an artist. He was pleased with David's paintings, so David painted.

Mike was the peacekeeper in his family. Everyone loved him. He was so sweet he could smooth over any situation. If

there was a problem he would come up with a solution. He never let them down — except he secretly started smoking marijuana behind the garage everyday after school before everyone got home. When I met him, he was a much loved and revered husband and father who seemed too good to be true. He always did and said the right thing, was never really disagreeable, and just so easygoing. His wife was happy except for one thing: she accidentally found a bag of marijuana in his car. On top of that, when she confronted him about it, Mike said it was his friend Tony's. The wife called Tony, and guess what? It wasn't his. Turns out Mike had pretty much perfected a secret underground life for himself where he did things he "wasn't allowed to."

I'm only one therapist. Every therapist — and there are lots of us — has these stories.

Making Space For Your Partner

So what do you do about emotional incest in your own relationship? This is a huge problem, because your partner has lost years and years of necessary self development and self-definition. He can grow beyond the emotional incest (as outlined in the men's side of the book) and you can help him. You can't do the work for him — SELF-defining has to come from the SELF — but you can create a loving, safe environment that encourages his work. Do not make decisions for him that he can — and needs to — make on his own. You can also remind him in *a loving voice*: I am not your mother/father. I am not your enemy. I am not against you. I am for you. I have space for you. I do not want to control you. I am on your side.

Your partner will not believe these words or concepts at first. You will have to say them over and over and over again. He has learned that loving or being loved means his *true self* and/or his *whole self* cannot be present. You need to keep reinforcing that that isn't true

anymore. That as an ADULT and in this marriage, his true self can come out and is welcome. He will test you by throwing out lots of false selves. Acting out. Try not to react but respond to this. "I love you and I know you don't know that in your core. You are a good person. And capable. And competent. You can figure this out."

So Much Fear

Every single person I have worked with who has emotional incest in his history — every single person without exception — expresses fearing that their partner won't like "the real me." They feel their partner fell in love with "the act" and wants that person — not me. "What if she doesn't like me?" or "What if she doesn't want this new me?" is going on for your partner. He is terrified that you will reject him. He is hyper-vigilant, looking for any signs of — even a hint of — rejection on your part. After all, his whole childhood was marked by being loved for his "act." How could he believe that you could REALLY love him? It is excruciatingly scary for him to even entertain the idea. He'd just as soon not do it actually. One of my clients told me, "I'm like a crab that hides under a rock. I've been under that rock a LONG time. I want to come out, but I'm scared. What if I get stepped on? What if I'm ugly? What if I'm not good enough? You've convinced me to venture out, but I'm telling you, I'm ready to run right back any second." I believe him. This is your husband. He is looking for any little excuse to run back under the rock and hide. Try not to give it to him.

River Water

But when is enough enough? Again, so much depends on if you are seeing effort on your husband's part and if you are seeing progress. Effort alone without progress is a waste. It's the difference between water in a river and water in a lake. The water in the lake is constantly moving around but not going anywhere. You want river water. You

want to know he's getting somewhere. I've outlined some very specific behaviors for your husband to take in the men's side of this book (like going to New Warrior, like going to a therapist who understands emotional incest, etc.). You need to be watching, observing whether those things are happening. I will say progress is slow when dealing with emotional incest. At first. It takes that tremendous energy to make the train wheels turn half an inch. However, like the train, once your husband really starts going, progress will be faster and faster with less and less effort. Watch and see if that's happening. Don't nag and see: watch and see. I always suggest giving yourself a time frame: 3 months, 6 months, 9 months, whatever you're comfortable with. Don't spend your lifetime waiting for change. You really ought to be able to see at least some progress in self-definition by six months. This is critical because if your husband does not self-define, he will not be able to be authentically emotionally available to you.

Chapter 8

Three Choices

You really have three choices with your relationship: leave it, keep it the same, or make it better.

Keeping It the Same

If you are reading this book because your partner is emotionally unavailable, I do not recommend keeping your relationship the same. You have probably experienced enough loneliness and pain for a life-time already. It's time for a change. Change means you are going to have to do things differently, say things differently, even think things differently. I am amazed sometimes when people come to me for couple's counseling and have no intention of changing. They want their PARTNER to change but have given little consideration to doing any changing themselves. Yes, your partner has to change, too, but you cannot expect any deep-level change in your relationship to hap-pen if you remain the same.

So it's important to ask yourself, do I want things to stay the same? Am I happy with the ways things are? Do I get my needs met? Does my partner? If the answer is a resounding no, I don't want things to keep being the same, then you have to begin to "call yourself" on your "same" behavior. This involves a very personal, honest relationship with yourself. It's an internal process where you get into a habit of asking yourself: is this behavior the same or is it different? At every

crossroads you ask yourself: am I doing what I always do? Am I saying the same old, same old maybe just with different words? Am I still inside the box or am I stepping outside of it to have a different angle to consider? You must develop the skill of being able to see when YOU are encouraging your relationship system to remain at status quo. And believe me, you will do that. We all do. It's normal and our natural resistance to change. However, you've got to catch yourself in the act and remind yourself of your goal: to get out of "the same." The same doesn't work. It hasn't thus far, at least, so choose something different. Choose a behavior that is more effective.

Leave It

Leave it means breaking up, moving out, getting a divorce, ending the relationship because it doesn't work. In general I do not believe divorce is the answer. But sometimes, it is. My mother divorced my alcoholic, sociopathic father when I was three. It was THE best thing that ever happened to me in my life. I believe it saved my life. If you are in a destructive relationship do not think you are doing your kids any favor by staying. So many people stay together "for the kids," when the kids would be remarkably better off being taken out of the war zone. Being raised by one parent who isn't frequently crying or raging (hurricaning) or in active addiction, is much better for the children than being raised by two parents who are at emotional war with each other.

My rule of thumb is, if you cannot make the relationship better (not completely 100 percent healed, but BETTER) within 6–12 months, and keeping it the same is not an option because of the destructiveness of it (including lack of loving behaviors), then leaving it is better than staying. My preference, of course, is making the relationship better, but if this is not going to happen, difficult as it is, leaving is better than staying in the same destructive quagmire for years. Leaving is never easy. It involves great loss and grieving. But this pain, though intense, is temporary (it lasts 6–12 months usually) compared to the chronic

pain and heartache of a lifetime in a relationship that is frustrating and unfulfilling and damaging to you and your children.

So, if you have honestly worked on making the relationship better and that didn't happen, and keeping the relationship the same is no longer an option for you, then leaving is the choice you are facing. In order to leave you must do two things. First, really choose it. Decide. Make a private, conscious decision not based on what other people think but on what YOU think. Can you say: "I've had enough of keeping it the same. I'm done. I want something different for my life"? If so, then you can DECIDE to leave. Second, and this is the most important behavior you can do once you've made this decision: don't look back. I'm reminded of the Biblical story in Genesis of Sodom and Gomorrah where Lot is told to take his family, flee the city, and warned not to look back. Lot's wife, of course, looks back, and is turned into a pillar of salt. So it is with leaving a marriage. Don't look back, or you'll turn into a pillar of salt. You must look forward. Keep your eyes on the road straight ahead of you looking forward to emotional serenity, looking forward to being loved by another, looking forward to good things coming your way, looking forward to not being lied to anymore, etc. Do not look back. Keep remembering that keeping it the same is no longer an option. You deserve more. You deserve better. Life is short. Move on to your next chapter, because it's going to be a good one.

Postscript

The looking back (when you turn to a pillar of salt) is usually about second guessing yourself. Did I try hard enough? Long enough? Maybe I should have done, said, thought . . . Be careful not to "should" on yourself. If you have put forth an honest, loving effort for a 6–12 month period where you've pretty much cleaned up your side of the street (remember you cannot do this completely without your partner's help, so just that you have cleaned it up as much as you can), and your partner is still coming home drunk or not coming home, or your part-

ner remains non-communicative and is truly not interested in changing that, or your partner lies to you, or your partner is still working 7 days a week, 12 hours a day or whatever the behavior is that makes him unavailable, then you've done enough. You've tried enough. You've given enough. Don't look back. Look forward. A better life awaits you.

Making the Relationship Better

Really this whole book has been about making the relationship better. Provide safety, love, and healing to your partner. Clean up your side of the street. Stop hurricaning. Be honest with yourself. Come to know yourself and your games. Have appropriate boundaries. Make conscious choices. Grow up. You are not a victim. Take responsibility. Learn to love.

And that's what it all comes down to: love. Your life will get better if you consciously choose to love yourself and your partner. Love yourself enough to settle for nothing less than emotional availability from him. Love him enough to be kind to him even in his brokenness and in his process of learning emotional availability. Love yourself and him enough to honestly look at your three choices: to make the relationship better, to keep it the same, or to leave. Don't keep it the same: life is too short and you both are too valuable. It's time for a change. May clarity be yours.

Recommended Reading

Adult Children of Alcoholics by Janet Geringer Woititz

Anger Busting 101 by Newton Hightower

Boundaries by Henry Cloud and John Townsend

Driven To Distraction by Edward Hallowell and John Ratey

The Emotional Incest Syndrome by Pat Love

Feel the Fear and Do It Anyway by Susan Jeffers

Getting the Love You Want by Harville Hendrix

The Life You've Always Wanted by John Ortberg

Man's Search for Meaning by Viktor E. Frankl

The Prophet by Kahlil Gibran

Seven Habits of Highly Effective Families by Stephen R. Covey

Too Good to Leave, Too Bad to Stay by Mira Kirshenbaum

Upon This Rock: Miracles of a Black Church by Samuel G. Freedman

What to Say When You Talk to Yourself by Shad Helmstetter

Who Moved My Cheese? by Spencer Johnson

Index